Revolution, American Style

CHANDLER & SHARP PUBLICATIONS IN
POLITICAL SCIENCE

General Editor: Victor Jones

Revolution, American Style

The Nineteen-Sixties and Beyond

Paul N. Goldstene

Chandler & Sharp Publishers Inc.
Novato, California

Library of Congress Cataloging-in-Publication Data

Goldstene, Paul N., 1930–
    Revolution, American style: the nineteen-sixties and beyond /
Paul N. Goldstene.
        p.   cm. — (Chandler & Sharp publications in political
science)
    Includes bibliographical references (p.   ) and index.
    ISBN 0-88316-566-X
    1. United States—Politics and government—1945–1989. 2. United
States—Politics and government—1989– 3. United States—Economic
conditions—1945– 4. United States—Social conditions—1945–
5. Revolutions—United States. I. Title.
JK1726.G65 1997
320.973'09'045—dc21   97-18236

Printed on acid-free paper according to the guidelines for permanence and
durability of the Committee on Production Guidelines for Book Longevity
of the Council on Library Resources.

Edited by Jonathan Sharp.
Cover design and production by Joel Friedlander Publishing Services.
Book design and composition by Page One Graphics/David Nishikawa.

For Nettie, Ben, and Gene,
and for memories

"We can never be born enough."

". . . the essential power of man striving energetically for its object."

Karl Marx

Contents

Acknowledgments

To write is to incur debts which, however unpayable, must at least be recognized. Anyhow, if such a rule is not universal, it is certainly applicable here.

Regarding the actual production of this book, the chore of typing seemingly endless and indecipherable attempts at it fell to Ellen Tani, who once again demonstrated that her knack for transforming weird conglomerations of elocution and verbal jig-saw puzzles into usable drafts is nothing short of remarkable. The inevitable typographical and page-design quandaries were resolved by David H. Nishikawa, whose patience and skill are much appreciated, while Joel Friedlander and John A. Dibs crafted the cover design and index with an impressive proficiency.

Carolyn D. Hopkins proved crucial to my coping with an array of complications which infiltrated the composition of the "Appendix" and "Notes." Further thanks in reference to this are due to John P. Carlson, as well as to Elsa Favilla, who also offered sound advice on a number of matters of syntax and grammar, and even ventured to make sense of a scattered rendition of what became this volume. The chair of my department, Jean E. Torcom, engaged in a tacit—and very welcome—willingness to fail to notice my incessant demands on office expenses and personnel. Heather L. Muller came to grips with this effort in one of its sundry disguises, helped with certain esoteric problems of research and, along with Arthur H. Williamson, was of substantial assistance in the pursuit of an item which necessitated stumbling around in and, ultimately, through William J. Sullivan, Jr., a scholarly understanding of the German language. In addition, Ric Brown and Donald P. Zingale managed to acquire some financial aid for this work, an achievement facilitated by John T. Manns and Vicki Pearson-Rounds.

More than a few others read the manuscript, in whole or in

part, at different stages of its troubled career. I owe a great deal to their criticisms and, not surprisingly, to their being adept at reacting kindly. These include Terrell Carver, William A. Dorman, Robert J. Donovan, Bahman Fozouni, Heaven C. Gainsburgh, William Head, Donna Hoenig-Couch, Wilson Carey McWilliams, Sylvester M. O'Reilly, Ian C. Padilla, Jill M. Sanguenetti, Norman Solomon, Rick Tilman, and Douglas L. Ward. Beyond this, Mina B. Robbins made her way through a rather adolescent phase of this book as well as the page proofs but, most essentially, was persistent in her personal support. The latter is true, as has become habitual, of Harriette Warner, although I am aware that my publication rate does not satisfy her well-articulated inclinations. My editor, Jonathan Sharp, was a fan of this venture from its incipient emergence and, in light of my perverse reflexes, may be pleased to discover that his cogent—and always understated—recommendations are largely incorporated.

There are invariably people who are instrumental to the search for formulation, modification, and meaning that accompanies the long march of writing. Indeed, in a vital sense, they come to be collaborators. While still struggling to identify a unifying argument, I shared my hunches with T. Eugene Shoemaker, who effectively commented on what was already scrawled and, as usual, could perceive the possibilities within a confusing mélange of vague and random ideas. Catherine Nelson contended with more than one of many variations on the theme, responded in a positive and insightful manner, additionally urging that the relevance and tone of the 1960s be elaborated and made more central, an astute suggestion which, I suspect, yielded a sharper focus and magnified coherence. After grappling with some of the anticipatory ramblings, Neal Turner pondered several of the more complete manuscripts, conveying an insistent enthusiasm for the historical and social-psychological content which, one way or another, we discussed at considerable length. My debate with Michael F. Singman about what may be the deeper constituents of the

American political culture has been ongoing for many years and, regardless of our agreements and differences, he confronted each draft with pertinent thoughts about substance, was, as expected, extremely incisive on issues of consistency and voice, and talked me into according more attention to those particular requirements of the academy which I am evidently disposed to ignore. Teresa M. Derichsweiller supplied me with a discrete species of pencil that is quite difficult to come by and which I apparently cannot squander reams of paper without, arranged for copies as the work went through the long process of revision, and reacted to the changes with sensitive editorial input while riding herd on me to insure that this not become "another academic book"—a contribution which, undoubtedly, had a saluatory effect on the outcome.

My family, of course, played a pivotal role. I am grateful to Jami Warner Goldstene for lending her expertise to this enterprise. James N. Goldstene cheered me on after perusing a bit of the early meanderings, read the page proofs, as did Claire C. Goldstene, and both, in alliance with Beth M. Goldstene, became an important force for keeping me reasonably centered in what, within an era of science, many might agree is the real world.

Finally, Ellen F. Goldstene read some of the preliminary jottings, employed her acumen for style to make a useful analysis of an initial version of the "Introduction" and of the final draft of the manuscript itself, and was plainly indispensable by abetting the undue preoccupation which attends my inexplicable need to try to make sense of the modern condition by writing about it, doing this with much humor, as well as with a stubborn confidence in the result. Since two of my previous literary adventures are—partially and fully—dedicated to her, this one is not. Yet, it well could be.

So, if any who are mentioned finds a degree of merit in this work, perhaps my obligations can be considered, to some extent, as redeemed.

Revolution, American Style

Introduction: The Confluence of Attitude and "Methodology"

America, we are incessantly informed, is in the midst of or, perhaps, emerging from the Reagan "revolution" which, allegedly, is merely one expression of a more expansive "conservative revolution." Yet the mantle of "revolution" is frequently claimed by those who perceive the ex-President and his ideological compatriots as "counterrevolutionary." In a possibly more profound sense, José Ortega y Gasset contends that Western civilization has been in "revolution" for the past three centuries:[1] a civilization presently subsumed by the technological, scientific, and computer "revolutions," which are either participants in this greater "revolution"—or are not—and which manifest a postindustrial extension of the industrial "revolution"—or do not.

Albert Camus extols the rebel and abhors the "revolutionary";[2] Erich Fromm proposes the exact opposite;[3] but what they favor and what they oppose are virtually the same. Recent years have witnessed the "revolution" of higher expectations and the "revolution" of lowered expectations. To the minds of some, Nazism and fascism are the most crucial "revolutionary" developments of the century. Many prefer "communism," even as commercial products proudly announce themselves to be "revolutionary." There is, of course, the sexual "revolution," not to be confused with the gender "revolution." Those who determine the foreign policy of the United States advocate an array of "revolutions" and resist others, concurrently lauding "revolution" and despising it amidst a tortured cacophony of pronouncement and behavior. The word abounds and coherence fails while a myopic preoccupation with "revolution" saturates the political reflexes of the nation.

To be sure, we could get rid of the word. But another would

1

be quickly invented because that which the appellation is intended to convey is not likely to suddenly disappear. "Revolutions," Marx insists, "are the locomotives of history." This might be true. In any event, whether directly or by implication, a serious attempt to comprehend the human experience will probably run into their substantive realities.

For the thinkers of ancient Athens, at least for those who attain major influence in the subsequent Western world through the incorporation of a particular set of their ideas by a long-dominant Catholic Church in Europe, revolution is understood in its literal sense of revolving, of going around. However, the classical perception of cycles of illusionary change which necessitate the expenditure of great effort to go nowhere—bringing with them only devastation and dislocation within endlessly repetitive stages of rise and fall, "turning the tables" merely to inevitably return to a prior condition—is no longer satisfactory. Since the Enlightenment—if not earlier—revolution becomes "social revolution": a designation vitally imbued with a notion of human progress. The debate accordingly shifts to what may or may not actually be progressive, as well as to whether such a projection is feasible or a delusion which surpasses the capacities of human nature to attain.

Needless to say, it is revolution within this context that has inspired and terrified millions of people throughout the past three centuries, becoming an abiding concern of world-historical significance. Yet this does not mean, as some would argue, that social revolution is a uniquely modern phenomenon. It simply suggests that the conception of social revolution affords a new prism through which to try to view certain pivotal realities of human history which cannot be ignored.

Here, as in any scholarly field, specific works, whatever their actual merit, are held to be indispensable. This is an honor currently bestowed upon the efforts of Crane Brinton, Samuel P. Huntington, and Theda Skocpol—along with those of a very few more. Indeed, the essential promulgations of Huntington about revolutions congeal into a conceptual framework which has become almost mandatory if an attempt to address the subject is to command intellectual respect.

Revolutions, Huntington propounds, or "what others have called great revolutions, grand revolutions, or social revolutions," must "be distinguished from insurrections, rebellions, revolts, coups, and wars of independence." Thus, the famous formulation that "a revolution is a rapid, fundamental, and violent domestic change in the dominant values and myths of a society, in its political institutions, social structure, leadership, and government activity and policies." Moreover, revolutions witness "the rapid expansion of political consciousness and the rapid mobilization of new groups into politics at a speed which makes it impossible for existing political institutions to assimilate them." Importantly, for Huntington, quoting Carl J. Friedrich, "revolutions, in the grand sense, are . . . 'a peculiarity of Western culture'" or, more precisely, "the ultimate expression of the modernizing outlook, the belief that it is within the power of man to control and change his environment and that he has not only the ability but the right to do so."[4]

The empirical problems with this are abundant. If Huntington is correct in asserting that a revolution comprises a fundamental transformation in the prevailing values, myths and, finally, consciousness of a society and, by extension, that a social revolution has occurred when this takes place among a critical mass of a population, he is on shakier ground when he holds that revolution is strictly a modern development, by which he means the movement of societies from agrarian to industrial configurations. And, regardless of whether either of these propositions is right or wrong, transitions in "the dominant values and myths in a society" are never "rapid" in any empirically verifiable sense, and the causes of these transitions are not "violent," although persistent violence is likely to further entrench people into the habitual and familiar. What

kind of change would be considered "fundamental" is not
made clear, but it is unlikely that what is fundamental in an
established order will change quickly, and a "rapid expansion
of political consciousness" on an aggregate scale is historically
improbable, however it may sometimes appear to those involved.[5]

Still, few in the social sciences would dispute the efficacy of
Huntington's position: and, even when some seem to dis-
agree, they typically accept the content, if not the vocabulary,
of his suppositions while quibbling only on their edges. There
are, admittedly, differences in emphasis and nuance. Skocpol,
for instance, surmises that governments themselves are more
critical to contemporary revolutions than is generally acknowledged: a reflection of the fact that revolutions have become
less discretely "domestic" as the influence of foreign regimes
becomes increasingly common. This has been well understood
in reference to the unintended consequences of war. But now,
it is maintained, the transnational character of revolution is
amplified by more intense economic connections among national systems,[6] presumably a result of advanced technological
sophistication, especially that of mass communication. It follows that the contagion of revolution is a much greater factor
than ever before in human history as the role of nation-states
as autonomous "actors" within an international arrangement
effectively diminishes.

Furthermore, for Huntington, as for Crane Brinton
previously, and for most currently respected writers on revolution, all revolutions—and, it would appear, all politics—articulate the competition, alliance, and perceived success and
discontent among elites which, from time to time, engage in a
struggle for the temporary support of fickle populations. Accordingly, while Charles Tilly criticizes Huntington for failing
to sufficiently focus on those groups most instrumental to
revolution, along with, extrapolating from this, the organiza-
tional realities which help to make them instrumental; and
Ted Robert Gurr emphasizes the goals of these groups in

terms of "relative deprivation"; it is characteristically attested that revolutions compose volatile changes in basic societal values brought about by elites pursuing what they ascertain to be their own benefit.[7]

Skocpol shares this view yet, sympathetic to a Marxian approach, she is also amenable to the notion that revolutions do not come exclusively from "above" but are sometimes generated "from below,"[8] perceiving the "masses" as more important than is usually allowed, and inferring that greater attention should be paid to mass recruitment by elites. In addition, Brinton holds to the classical conviction that nothing meaningful is changed by the convoluted history of revolutionary episodes, even as he strangely suggests that the industrial revolution might be transforming the world;[9] for Huntington revolutions are purely manifestations of contemporary transitions from agrarian to industrial economic orders;[10] while Skocpol ultimately affirms that a broader distribution of power and authority might be an actual outcome of a revolution.[11]

Nonetheless, whatever their disagreements, it is the similarities among the leading writers on revolution which remain conceptually controlling. There is a consensus about the "facts" that revolutions demand organization and leadership and, most centrally, that they are "rapid" and "violent" eruptions which disturb for an identifiable and historically brief time the normal consistencies of systemic existence. Thus revolutions are conceived of as isolated episodes; not as disturbances that may disclose a larger process; and patently not as a process themselves—a perspective which has dominated the West since 1917.

Of greater theoretical influence, however, is the notable absence of dispute about what composes a legitimate analytic approach. Despite a bit of conjecture by Brinton and Huntington about the relationship of contemporary industrialization to revolution, along with a few comments by Huntington about the ideology that motivates industrialization and, by Brinton, about the correlation of revolutions, not so much with the apprehension of immediate monetary interests, but with the expectation by discrete factions of future financial opportunities[12]—conjectures which barely touch on these is-sues—there is no evident attempt to explain why revolutions occur. The preference is to describe and to separate and di-vide these descriptions into an arrangement of categories, thereby establishing a taxonomic structure within which the categories are then connected, disconnected, and connected again, maybe in a somewhat different way.

Hence, while a presiding concern about revolution is en-demic to the contemporary world, and as the implications and inferences of this concern reverberate through its political re-alities, any concerted effort to move toward an explanation of revolution is exceedingly rare in works that supposedly deal with the phenomenon. In short, the search for an adequate theory is an enterprise in which specialists on revolution hardly demonstrate a noticeable interest.

There are probably reasons for this. Certainly, data gather-ing is traditionally applauded by the academic community; enunciating categories sounds "scientific"; and within a social science that has come to confuse "rigor" for empiricism, much attention to description and, more pointedly, to the collection and categorization of what is described, emerges as a profes-sional requirement. The same reflex applies to the realm of theory, wherein the accepted role of the academy becomes one of compiling the thoughts of others or, at most, interpret-ing and criticizing them as—it must be granted—is being done here.

Plainly, not to theorize is to largely avoid the risk of being refuted: it is also to circumvent the charge of "reductionism," a trait which is inherent in the very act of theorizing. These emanate as the unstated but formal components of intellec-tual credibility. As a consequence, to write a great deal while saying not much about causality is the academic equivalent of being politically correct. It is, indisputably, the recommended road to professional success.

A few years ago, in his farewell address as president of the American Political Science Association, Theodore J. Lowi bemoaned the absence of large ideas in the discipline of political science as well as the reluctance of its practitioners to speak truth to power and, even worse, to become intellectuals by speaking truth to themselves.[13] This is a telling depiction of the current state of the political-science profession, one which is especially rampant in the subfield of revolution. It should encourage Lowi to think about what the more-prestigious graduate schools look for in regard to the theoretical dispositions of their applicants. He might discover that people reasonably content with the status quo are not inordinately motivated to truly investigate the foundations of its existence.

Such would be a finding which cannot be considered remarkable. "With a few outstanding exceptions, social scientists are essentially apologists for and not critics of the existing social system. This can be so because, unlike the natural sciences, their results are of little value for the functioning of society. On the contrary, erroneous results and superficial treatment have a useful function as ideological 'cement,' while the truth is, as always, a threat to the status quo."[14] It ought to be noted, moreover, that the most influential expositers of this obfuscating art are generally financed in relationship to the subtlety of their expression.

Anyhow, whether the resistance to theoretical creativity exposes an ideological ambition to put social science at the disposal of the operative order; or a desire to attain academic respectability by avoiding matters which may be complicated, and, accordingly, subject to the accusation of reductionism and, therefore, intellectually risky to delve into; or the associated policies of recruitment and reward within the important graduate schools; or all of these as a totality, what multiplies are works replete with description and a subsequent "analysis" which is little more than a taxonomy of this description. The result is an "information" industry that is avidly focused on tinkering with categories while discouraging a level of theoretical speculation which may be appropriate to the scope and texture of what is purportedly being studied.

Because categories are required to be what they are, and cannot be other than what they are, this must produce a portrait of human history as static, while an analysis of the frozen result is defined as the most advanced achievement of "social science." In this manner process becomes "events" and a seizure of political authority becomes a "revolution." This is testified to by an impressive volume of professional literature that claims to expound upon the process of revolution while carefully nullifying any real hunches about causality and, it must follow, any actual attempt to arrive at those glimpses of such a process which a theoretical effort might afford.

Huntington does draw a distinction between "political theory" which, he argues, is pertinent to the study of revolution, and historical theory, which he declares is not.[15] Yet to advance a theory of revolution open to the publicly accessible empirical evidence necessitated by science is, implicitly or otherwise, to engage in a theory of history. Not surprisingly, for example, revolutions are always discussed against a background of "political forces," "economic forces," or what Huntington himself finds to be "a new social force . . . or combination of social forces,"[16] or what has somewhere been referred to as "the slow rhythms of our planet."[17] Each of these is a synonym for historical forces and, as such, they introduce the very "historical theory" which Huntington alleges is of no real assistance when trying to identify the driving elements of revolution. Those who ponder the subject might do well to realize this, and to attend to the human substance that the revolutionary process may represent.

Still, nothing could be further from the predilections of the "experts" on revolution. They prefer to chronicle "occurrences"; and, in their most expansive reaches of intellectual daring, to categorize these occurrences; and then to pronounce upon and, occasionally, debate about how certain instances of them fit or do not fit into a perspective wherein the human psyche is fixed by an a priori assertion of the categories. Thus the experience and possibilities of vast multitudes of people are circumscribed through categorical definition and, by extension, revolutionary transformations are disassociated from historical motion.

Of course, unless one propounds an abstract force beyond the influence of human will and action, to enter the thicket of historical forces is to get into messy stuff—much of which might not easily lend itself to categorization. It is to try to grasp the way people in the aggregate are likely to behave and to speculate about why they do; to glimpse the contradictions which accompany human inclination and ambition; to come to grips with the need to fabricate and create, with the yearnings for liberty as an escape from power and for freedom as public power and effect, along with the etiology of those perceptions which induce values, attitudes, and controlling agreements about existence and opportunity. All of this is found in revolutions, perhaps revealing an evolving reality that applies to individuals as well as to populations: an insistent movement which reaches far back to the emergence of the species. It might even indicate that process and not stability is the normal condition of human beings and, hence, of their history.

These are difficult and pervading concerns, and revolution is a difficult and pervading matter. Aside from the work of Gurr, which possesses theoretical value, but which is more directed to the constituents of social stability than to revolution, among contemporary writers, Hannah Arendt is one of the few who attempts to develop an authentic theory of revolution[18] precisely because she is determined to grapple with the problem of historical forces. And the degree to which Arendt relies on the more sweeping ideas of two thinkers as apparently disparate as Tocqueville and Marx is suggestive, regardless of how much the influence of either, especially of Marx, might be denied. A reading of Tocqueville, once we get beyond the pithy little homilies about the United States which have attained such great popularity, and into the implicit and, at times, explicit view of history behind them, is theoretically instructive. So is a reading of Marx, less for the well-attended domain of mode of production and class struggle, and more for his contentions about the unity of opposites which permeates a historical materialism within the instruments of production: contentions upon which his political, social, and economic arguments are predicated. Both infer that revolutions are not momentary and unrelated episodes, but an inexorable ingredient of the human condition, and that to address "grand revolutions" while claiming to be "scientific" by avoiding the grand theory which the subject calls for is, finally, to be scientifically delinquent and misleading.

Nevertheless, Tocqueville and Marx are commonly viewed as "unscientific." Possibly, this is why their formulations cannot be ignored—and why reams of commentaries have been written about them—even by social scientists. The actual reason, however, is that each is willing to take on the opaque complexities of historical forces. It is this which allows Tocqueville to offer theoretical statements about the expansion of democracy as a linear and global reality. A similar willingness permits Marx to theorize in terms of historical stages brought about by the dialectical motion of a scientific and technological progression, which is the universal precondition of human realization through a coalescence of material abundance with unalienated labor and political equality. If Tocqueville is more subtle and Marx more overt; if Tocqueville worries about what is stirring while Marx applauds; if I herein agree less with Tocqueville than with Marx, is not the issue. They—along with others—write in the best tradition of science because they apply the theoretical imagination to illuminate their attempts at explanation wherein the size of the ideas complies with the magnitude of the phenomena being explored. Only then do they proceed to worry or applaud.

That Tocqueville and Marx exceed description and categorization by entering the murky arena of hypothetical and, eventually, theoretical conceptions about causality—always the preliminary steps toward an empirical comprehension of what may actually exist—is precisely why they should be perceived as within the central tradition of science; "a search for universal generalizations"[19] that may provide clues to the causal connections among the apparently disconnected qualities of "events"; a goal which must suffuse any scientific effort. Whatever the sphere of inquiry, every working theorist approaches an assumed material universe on these terms. To be a card-carrying member of the scientific enterprise all that is demanded is to be open to the test of empirical evidence—as Tocqueville and Marx happen to be. But even if they are not, their arguments can certainly be employed by those who agree with such an epistemological commitment.

Description and categorization are necessary to the doing of theory, as is the accepted language of discourse. Yet, rooted in what is tentatively known about reality, it is speculation that propels the enormous theoretical influence of modern science; and it is notorious that these speculations often derive from unexpected places, advancing perception and predictability and, possibly, for political science, civic judgment. That theoretical propositions become plausible only when sustained by empirical verification is not in dispute, and the methodology of the scientific endeavor historically assures that many of these will provoke suitable attention.

In this regard, an emphasis on "methodology" is vital to confirmation, or the absence of it and, thereby, to the question of plausibility. Nonetheless, methodology and data without theory produce a world of nonsense or, at best, trivia, because only theory, explicit or implied, can make sense of data. The great advances in the history of science are not instigated by those who verify or, as social scientists enamored with Karl R. Popper would prefer, "falsify," but by those who observe a cognitive dissonance within the established theories, and who effectively encourage paradigm shifts with new, and usually unacceptable, surmises which often yield greater explanatory power.[20]

Indisputably, there are theories which have exhausted their capacity to contribute much to explanation. These frequently become assumptions, usually articulated as "common sense"— or what John Kenneth Galbraith usefully labels "the conventional wisdom"[21]—which increasingly interfere with further comprehension by unduly confining the parameters and depth of what is being investigated. For this reason alone, the need for more data cannot be ignored. However, the very selection of data is a manifestation of theory and, after the initial impact of a material condition, data themselves result from speculation inasmuch as "evidence" cannot escape the influence of those preceding presuppositions and assumptions about cosmological and epistemological considerations which, when not stated, are invariably implicit.

Patently, the construction of theory is the "iffy" side of science: one may be "wrong" on a rather large scale. This is more likely in the social sciences than in the natural sciences because, as Einstein pointed out, the social sciences are "the hard sciences"; the relevant variables are much more numerous than in the natural sciences; and empirical support, or lack of support, for any formulation, is far slower to accumulate.

So too are the accolades which the intellectual community might choose to award. But, since prior to Socrates and Heraclitus, the history of the speculative foundations of scientific discovery is not a history of accolades—or even of professional respectability. It is instead a saga of the human imagination and its leaps into the unknown and what ramifies from this cannot simply be defined away as improper questions for science. In fact, for the social sciences the present price of a respectability gained by narrowing the range of exploration is to promulgate a view of reality that flies in the face of modern scientific perception: an array of theories which, at its core, apprehends a unity of natural forces that infer a continual pressure for process, motion and, ultimately, transformation. As a parallel, any attempt to scientifically decipher revolution must move toward sequential approximations of the inclusive and unifying forces within the human experience.

In the final analysis, science is a value system—and, because this necessitates authority, an order of politics—wherein those who do science have to function. Yet, on a deeper level, science is actually a way of approaching life, a search for the self and, by extrapolation, for insight into the greater world and the universe. It is, therefore, to be expected that a scientific quest for the elusive texture of revolution will drive the inquiry toward the more profound realms of human motivation, and those who would pursue the subject from within the tradition of science must walk the trail where it leads. To not do this is to in effect deny that such a science is feasible; or, probably more accurately, desirable.

It is an annoying complication that among the vast numbers of people who exist in our own time we only know ourselves—perhaps a little—and a very few others—maybe a little better. We are stuck with generalizing from this, an activity which is always personal,[22] and to call it "social science" does not make it into something else. Indeed, the transition from the private to the quantum is the basis of human knowledge and, when accompanied by an openness to the strictures of empirical evidence, this becomes the generic composition of any theoretical venture compatible with the scientific enterprise. That the personal character of theory is more visible when we face the opaque qualities of revolution reveals a difference merely of degree, not of kind: a reflection of the fact that the operative variables appear as more compelling and volatile than may be usual. In this sense, as John Dunn points out, "whether favourable or hostile . . . the value-free study of revolution is a logical impossibility for those who live in the real world," and "that to entertain any theory about the meaning of revolution . . . is to assume a political posture,"[23] to become actively engaged in the subject itself. To the extent that this is true, the position being taken must affect the form and voice of the presentation.

So, while to many trained in the social sciences it may seem otherwise, what follows is a serious effort to propose a theory about the human forces that energize the motion of revolution, especially as these have found expression in the United States—and to try to do this within the ambience and agreements that constitute the scientific outlook. At least it is an effort to take a few steps in that direction. Accordingly, it comprises a speculative essay which asserts a connection to the theoretical tradition that infuses the history of science: a form of writing, within a technocratic age of "methodology" and "data," which is little understood and a bit arcane—if not nearly extinct. The motivations that drove the initial scribblings are unlikely to be of interest. However, they are crucial to the public purpose of the enterprise because they cogently inform the result.

Such, I suspect, is a purpose which falls into one of the two prevailing themes of political philosophy. The first is characteristically elitist, delineating what is wrong with the order of things and then offering to save all concerned through proper instruction: a how-to-do-it angle toward action in the polis. Americans who, until very recently, were typically devoid of any awareness of what might be the tragic dimensions of human history, have traditionally favored this angle—and, by and large, they still do. But it is conceivable to analyze a condition while offering no list of recommended solutions: implicitly professing the egalitarian claim that people in general possess the capacity—and ability—to rationally deal with the world to the degree that they empirically comprehend it. This is the angle taken here, one, it might be mentioned, that accords with those salient values and attitudes which epitomize the perspective of science.

Although this work is not about the 1960s, it tries to use as a touchstone what has become a tangible yearning among many to appreciate the revolutionary inclinations of that time and to identify their significance within the larger parameters of American history. As do all attempts to formulate theory in any field, it articulates that peculiar constellation of science fiction and autobiography which, when open to the stipulations of empirical evidence, might encourage some who confront it to perceive the possibilities of a material reality in a slightly different manner than they did before. Beyond this, it gladly leaves the issues of confirmation and rebuttal to others.

1. The "Silence" of the Nineteen-Fifties

Blowing cool.

Rogers. Shank. Mulligan. The Lighthouse in Redondo Beach. Exotic for us. Where we were. Listening to Chet Baker in the Rouge Lounge outside of Detroit. "The thrill is gone." The whisper of the fifties. "The thrill is gone." The role of the children is to replicate the fathers. "This is the end." Everybody knows what America's about, Buddy. "So why pretend?" If life seems stupid, have a beer. "And let it linger on?" Tough country, America. "The thrill is gone."

Events conspire. Thus do they mold the clay of human beings into a view of the world as it is and as it should be, no matter how myopic the perception or empty the norm. As with all generations, events conspired to shape us into a discrete entity, and to play us off against the events of preceding generations and of those which would follow.

References to generational perception, response, and prejudice are not unusual in the formulations of historical understanding. But no one speaks for a generation, not even for a segment of it. Indeed, as we scatter to other burdens and, perhaps, more mature concerns, all we want to speak for is ourselves. Yet the way we see the world is infused with the environment and sludge of our generational ooze, that milieu which produced the species of our time. In this sense, whenever we speak, no matter how personally, we speak for our generation, however such a reality may offend our individual sensibilities.

The power of generational agreement is, perhaps, best realized in middle or later age. That shared anguish of an interlude when crucial decisions are made; when fundamental directions are set; when the logic of choices arrived at or not

16

achieves motion and lasting effect. We all know the intrusive influence of generational affiliation, and we know it in a deeply personal way. There is always a generation gap. It is an essential fact of history.

But it is fallacious to ultimately conceive of history in generational terms, to ignore the paramount truth that the commonalities among all generations are inordinately more pervasive than the differences: that joy and folly and love and unacknowledged error and the yearning for an inner cohesion that accompanies the correct decision and the right action are the experience of all generations, and can't be the special property of one. In historical perspective, a generation is nothing. And yet, to really believe this is to affirm that life is nothing, because we largely live within the cloistered habitat of our generational associations and conditioning. And, as people actually exist, such associations and conditioning are vital since in a private way, in the only way we finally know, it is this which modulates the possibilities and limits of perception and response—a controlling variable that we share even with the enemies of our era, and that can't be shared even with the friends of another. We are unique. However, we are connected, because the story of our time can represent progress or regression only in relation to history itself. And it is this mix of the particular and the common that we must come to grips with if we are to attempt to comprehend the phenomenon of revolution.

Ours is a generation already written off as "silent," a generation that came to age as it retreated into a deadening conformity, too submerged and prosaic to even imagine the millennium that other generations eagerly pursued. Yes, we reflexively despised fascism, but we possessed neither the radicalism of the 1930s nor the liberal idealism of the early forties. Our political solidification came too late in the decade. We were, in fact, the generational backwash of large and exhausted movements.

In the years of our awakening consciousness the world was at war; the second war to end war of the twentieth century; the first truly world war of human history. We opposed Hitler as by instinct, as some would oppose the emotional echoes of his Romantic exhortations in the America that came later. For our generation, World War II loomed as the great narrative event: the great divider of generations in our part of the century. And, despite the horror of its actuality, the experience of the war contained an exhilaration, a positive particle that seemed to characterize the essence of the experience. Still, ours is a generation far from positive.

We are truly the children of the 1950s, our pervading and formative reality being a permeating anticommunism that enveloped the nation as a fog, choking out the light and any serious consideration of what might surpass that which already was; enfeebling conception and commitment; enfolding us in an insidious holding action against humanity and history. Now locked into a categorical cage by those who decide what history is, we are a generation dismissed. We are not of interest, least of all to ourselves. If there ever was a generation of political limbo, ours is it.

Dwight was in the White House and all was well with the world. Or so the world claimed: certainly the world that mattered. We were—we were told—the generation of Ike and prosperity and acquisitive striving and a barren suburbia and an absence of political vision and an attraction to serial barbecues and a patriotism which was never more than warmed-over platitudes choreographed by an array of mass media which was busy placating an insistent need for community. We were truly an American generation in what is truly the worst sense.

If the obvious event in our lives was World War II, the less obvious and more intractable fact was that those who preceded us and fought it were now in charge. Their central architecture, their major gift to our well-being, was the Cold War, an intellectual contraption in which they developed a

tremendous stake, a suffocation of creative political ideas typified by the vacuous platitudes it induced. It was the Cold War,
and the overt and subtle McCarthyism which it inherently represented, that subsumed our political meaning and matura-
tion. Not that we invented the Cold War or guided the twists
and turns of its tortured perceptions. But we lived within its
presence, finding our political selves on either side of a somehow declared line; as Dulles replaced Acheson and Marshall,
to be replaced by Herter and Rusk; as style changed and actuality remained rigidly in place.

Wherever we stood in regard to it, this line set the standard,
a standard to which we reacted and, by so doing, ceded to it
overwhelming power. Even we who opposed only in a private
manner, with little bravery and effect, except in kitchen arguments of great heat and profundity. We were, perhaps, slightly
more aware of the monolith of counterrevolution than those
who parroted the emerging platitudes of a corporatist liberalism. The truth, however, is that none of us saw the shadow too
well, and none of us really appreciated its primacy at all, because we failed to apprehend that the red-scare is critically a
part of the American psyche.

Whether one was an agent of McCarthyism, or of the as-
signed enemy, or of the middle that became suspect to both
sides, the price of our preoccupation was monumental and
is still being paid. Only later would new vistas begin to open,
only then would official America begin to take notice of
more expansive global forces and, maybe, of the probability
that every instance of discontent in the world is not a calcu-
lated affront to the classical free market of David Ricardo.
Still, we who knew the battles of the red-scare are actually
more than a little reluctant to leave it to the past. These
were battles that allowed us a semblance of self and purpose, and we resist throwing away our generational identity.
Those of us on the political Left, and I assume, on the
Right, and elsewhere, now grudgingly and haltingly come to
acknowledge new constellations of power and concern

which threaten to render us irrelevant. But in such a world we can't discover our political bearings, the direction of our integration and wholeness.

Nevertheless, if this uneasy exploration into a generational ethos is to reflect an attempt at honesty, I must protest against the connotation and mood of my own argument. Our generation didn't create Ike, and elect him, and feel comforted that America could serenely ignore its inner contradictions in the name of a Kansas Americanism; we didn't manufacture McCarthy; we didn't execute the Rosenbergs. It was not us who promulgated the Truman Doctrine and the Cold War, and ethnic quotas, and restricted neighborhoods, and the fear to think further than the truths established by authoritative pronouncement and innuendo. Yet—out of ignorance of who we really may be—we accept the verdict of the instant historians that we are implicated because we are the generation of quiet acceptance. We are part of the conspiracy to sabotage the American dream. In the age-old battle between the emergent and what already is, between life and form,[1] we award ourselves no part. Unwilling to break the mold and look into ourselves, we are ciphers in our own perceptions. We are the hollow men[2] of the twentieth century, lacking the depth to recognize the fact.

However, we are worth understanding because we are the seedbed of the decade of the sixties that only now is imposing its tenacious effects on America and the planet, even as the "Thermidor"[3] it evoked offers comfort to those who prefer things as they are, and as "the mammoth rests between his cyclonic dramas."[4] These are significant effects because they signal the beginning of a willingness to, perhaps, get beyond muckraking and "reform" and into the subtle power complexities of a postindustrial epoch. Within this context, if we weren't the first generation to attempt to comprehend, we were the first generation which glimpsed enough to be disturbed.

Despite teachers and books, we most directly learn from our generational peers: from each other as we respond to what appears to be the world. But our differences with other generations must finally be absorbed into similarities. Hence we begin to roam the past looking for the themes which reveal them, seeking a continuity larger than ourselves. This finds expression in a search for tradition; in a hunch that purpose is necessary to other than an animal existence; in a growing conviction that purpose of this kind is found only in the implicit direction—whether of repetition or a stipulated linear or dialectical progress—of history itself.

The content of tradition is primarily realized through abstraction. Yet we are never quite satisfied with this. All traditions must be made concrete by memories—of people and events—seldom known or experienced by us—people and events with whom and with which we identify and, by so engaging, become, along with those who write our history, part of the act of creating a tradition and transforming it.

Within any tradition, the defining parameters are generally agreed upon, although agreement is never absolute, and selection is finally a private matter amidst the persistent struggle for perception: a struggle which is really a quest for personal identity on a public scale. Embraced by the resulting tension, we listen for the rhythms of history, attempting to discover our invisible partners in the dance of existence.

Whatever the language, references, and nuances of a particular generation, it is this need for identity which becomes extrapolated into the perennial struggle between revolution and counterrevolution. And it is precisely in this regard that America is difficult to understand. The essential music of the country resounds as discord, and the partner in the national dance becomes a shadow associate—always there and always not—producing an industry of the mind ardently hunting for the "real America."

Such discord, of course, is usually attributed to the "plural-

istic" character of the order: an attribution which depicts an
arena wherein an array of "private" interests clamor for access
to a "public" state. With the theory of pluralism, the discord is
found to be normal. America becomes a mélange of "individuals"—or, in more sophisticated parlance, an aggregation of
groups, primarily economic—wherein there is no "public" but
only the terminology of a "public interest" presumably tossed
up from group dynamics and interaction. This becomes a nation without a country, a "community" as a figment of an
imagination that voices a human desire for limits which,
within the panorama of our politics, seldom seem to exist.
Here is what the liberal version of revolution supposedly promotes as the ideal "system": an ideal that neatly accords with
"market values" and that delights the conservative critique
which can happily surmise the presence of a creeping "anarchy" that must be controlled.

   Still, a "system" infers agreement; it conveys resolution, not
dilemma. And the fact is that all liberal portrayals of American
politics posit a set of ideological absolutes which function as
counterpoint and constraint, regulating the volatile diversity
of competition and alliance among interests as they maneuver
for policy advantage. However implicit and problematic to discern, these absolutes are the "system." They stipulate those
expected relationships and expectations which mandate the
accepted order of things.
   But ideological agreements are vague, and are often confused with myth—that which people think they believe but
don't act upon—and exactly where they come from remains
an extremely speculative consideration. Yet not to pursue the
basis of ideological agreement is to tacitly consent to the freez-
ing of a "system" as permanent and static. Motion can then
only occur within an a priori condition that is endemically
without motion and, accordingly, not subject to change in any
humanly important sense.[5] And it is this pluralistic conception
of an inherently stable America—and the fear of process its

approval signifies—which yields much that is crucial to the national ambience.

Of course, what is avoided is history and, along with it, any opportunity to evaluate the motivation behind those pivotal transformations which reveal the larger forces hidden within the urgently contested issues of immediate politics. It is to deny all theories about the consistencies and motion of the systemic transitions which epitomize the experience of the species. Indeed, it is to find irrelevant those permeating rhythms of perception, aspiration, and need which compose the texture of human power and, ultimately, the phenomenon of revolution.

To be sure, few of us thought about any of this very much. And when we did, our conclusions were quite otherwise. What we typically contended was that the real secret to stability and liberty in America is an abiding affection for the United States Constitution—and the division and separation of political authority which it defines and elaborates—as well as for the principles of due process of law which it allegedly contains. Accordingly, the argument affirmed, we possess the oldest continuing constitutional government in the world—and if the British are exempted because they failed to write their constitution into one preeminent document, and if the scattered vagaries of judicial review, which constitute the actual substance of the American Constitution, are ignored, what we claimed may be true. Presumably proposed was the central position of natural rights as they are translated into civil rights and liberties through the generic contract ratified in 1789, and which fuse an ex-colonial people into a coherent political order.

However, this was rhetoric that is subject to disturbing rebuttal. The survey data are stubborn and predictable. We seek cohesion in a Constitution, the Preamble to which announces a salient search for liberty and domestic tranquility, with little clue that these represent the language of incompatible doc-

trinal positions. We propound a love of "ordered liberty" with
no thought about the internal contradictions that confound
the conception. In any event, an affinity for the Bill of Rights
and the Civil War amendments wherein, with little exception,
the formal protections of individual rights reside, has never
been notable among the broad generality of the American
people—nor, to any impressive extent, among those who are
purportedly in charge. With an increasing emphasis on executive and judicial authority, such an affinity is even less directed
to the organization of government as manifested in the several
articles which compose the original document, and which express an essential distrust of the centralized authority of the
state. It is C. Wright Mills[6] who points out that we do not study
the American political system, we celebrate it. Yet that which
we celebrate is hardly real.

What this reflects is a confusion profoundly rooted in our
own past. Following the initial Puritan attempt to extend the
reach of dynasty, what came to North America with the great
English immigrations of the late-seventeenth and early-eight-
eenth centuries was John Locke. And the Lockian foundation
of the "American century"[7] persists. Along with its fiction of
successive contracts whereby people leave a state of nature,
producing a society and, eventually, a properly balanced civil
order, comes the mystification of property and a regime of
entrepreneurial elites ruling a system of equal financial opportunity. This is a vision predicated upon natural law as the
indisputable measure of all that is moral, true, and rational as
these cohere within, and literally, become, each other: and
upon natural rights, especially the right to and, finally, of
property, those central expressions of the laws of nature which
must be protected by the world of the "economic" checking
that of the "political."
  Therein announced is the liberal revolution and the en-
trance into history of "rational economic man," that great redundant catchphrase of the capitalist lexicon—a creature of

an insatiable material greed that is always at the highest level of intensity who must enter an automatic struggle for a profitable return among those rational enough to persevere in a free market. Thus articulated is an arena of winners and losers wherein only the inner self, and not a hierarchical structure into which one is born, can be blamed for personal monetary failure, and wherein each individual is released to pursue the wealth acquisition which signifies success. For the first time in its history, contends Adam Smith, humanity will experience a revolution of economic efficiency and, relative to its materialistic proclivities, even abundance. Or, after Robert Malthus and David Ricardo, at least a revolution of mitigated scarcity.

Lurking beneath all of this is the assumed reality of three distinct realms of human existence: the personal, the economic, and the political. These become abstractions that virtually ensnare the civic imagination in the United States. The likely tyranny of a "public" state is ultimately resisted by the countervailing effect of a competitive striving for profit within a "private" commercial aggregation which concurrently neutralizes all attempts to achieve a monopoly position because it prevents the attainment of market power. Moreover, a government, which is merely an "artificial" convention of human beings, can't claim authority over economics which are "natural" and thereby pursuant to the laws of nature. Beyond the minimal function of protecting the sanctity of contracts voluntarily entered into by parties that are often individual and— for the dominant element of the Federalist faction and its mercantilist successors, the building of a necessary material infrastructure—the accumulation of money is a matter which is conclusively "personal." Through a process of price competition among entrepreneurs who, by searching for the ratios between supply and demand in their efforts to maximize their financial holdings, are merely acting out the atomizing inclinations of the human personality, the wealth of nations is magnified and liberty is promoted. In this manner laissez-faire becomes natural law and the "pluralistic" outcome of the "revolution" of 1776 is ensured.

Here is a pervasive, if implicit, view about the relationship of property to power—and to the self. It is a tribute to the certainty that the inevitable corruptions of political authority and a consequent tyranny can be resisted only by the income distributions which must result from the release of the avaricious potentialities of human beings. Such is the liberal rendition of an "empire of reason,"[8] wherein the authority of the state reflects the alleged will of the sovereign people, a will which supposedly approximates natural law itself, and which therefore commands that government be comprised of the most rational and, hence, of those who are rich. What evolves is an order deriving from a perception of a species driven by the dark side of its nature: the passions that threaten tyranny and that must be restrained by elite opposing elite within a rational economic arrangement that serves the natural tendencies of human beings as well as the initial intentions of the social contract.

As an entrepreneurial appetite for economic power is confronted by an identical appetite among other participants in the market, so the tendency to become a tyrant through a monopoly of power is checked by the actions of others of a similar disposition: a classically liberal system within which "ambition must be made to counteract ambition,"[9] and faction to counteract faction. This extrapolation from competing business elites in the sphere of economics becomes manifest in competitive constitutional constraints among those same elites which properly govern in the sphere of politics. Only a combination of this kind releases the productive energies of the individual and proclaims the arrival of a republic.

Thus the habitual American agreements: a rational order of the financially "talented" within which, by fundamental assumption, all are not equal in acquisitive capacity. Predicated upon an understanding of human nature as a "possessive individualism"[10] that owes nothing of the self to society, the crux of the American constitutional idea is grounded in the conceptions and vocabulary of entrepreneurial wealth. This is opportunity as the right to "maximize utilities" through the pursuit of monetary gain, a presiding right which brings with it the acclaimed diversity of the "open society" and, most tangibly, an "interest group liberalism" which eventuates in rule by an appropriate meritocracy. Emanating from values and attitudes absorbed by those who lead as well as by those who follow, what is predominantly American finds realization in a conception of revolution as economics and in the political derivations of the intrinsic composition of the market. Hence, in the world of revolution American style, rights are that which relegate the individual to the traditional liberal realm of the private sphere of the personality. Or, more accurately, they subsume the realm of the personal into the realm of the economic through the translation of human rationality into financial acumen. What Marx will call "the cash nexus" prevails.

Plainly, the popular commitment to the Constitution varies with the perception—however arrived at, or manufactured—of the security of these radiating ideological considerations. Above all, there is property, the required adhesive between capitalism and the American understanding of constitutional government. Devolving from this connection, a culture of occasional constitutionalists emerges.

It follows that "parchment barriers"[11] hold Americans together only as long as they assure that property rights are preserved and, in the final analysis, promoted. But this is to be expected. Capitalism is the most profound political doctrine of the nation; a mode of production which presumably encourages, while it minimizes and, perhaps, obviates, the effect of the natural greed of people for money, status, and privilege; rendering impossible the phenomenon of market power and its translation into political, social, and economic suzerainty.

This is the ideological reality. It was certainly the perspective of the 1950s, a perspective that becomes most evident when material affluence and monetary security are perceived to be under assault. At these moments a traditional business consciousness overtly reasserts its easily acceptable dominance over the definition of the national will.

2. Capitalism as American Revolution

In the era of its formulation the capitalist pronouncement was revolutionary enough and, in fact, was as far as the technological forces of the time could actually extend. Serving what John Adams referred to as the *"passion for distinction,"*[1] as well as the projection of this passion into the rational activity of enhancing material production, the conception of "equal opportunity," releasing a maximization of individual utilities, or personal wealth, comprises the starting point of what is known as American political thought. Ramifying from the self-evident truths of natural law and natural rights, the great period of its articulation comes to dominate the world view of a people who will later consolidate into a nation.

Such is an ideological theme which actually finds its doctrinal source in British political ideas, especially those of a business liberalism. But, in the century leading up to the rebellion of 1775, an indigenous culture develops among the Europeans who are rapidly settling the Eastern seaboard of the middle of North America. Still largely British in outlook, the colonial experience nevertheless promulgates an emphasis on local authority which becomes institutionalized during the hundred years that London is ignoring its overseas interests: an emphasis which is distinctly foreign to the English political mind of that period—and now as well.

At the core of this formative emergence, even before many were aware of it, was a very human effort to find identity through a specific account of revolution. Herein is the basis of "American exceptionalism," the contention that the pluralism which emanated from their engagement in "free markets" disclosed that those who populated the British territories in North America were somehow superior to people in other parts of the known world.[2] Local supremacy and the principle of federalism—within the purview of a more traditional de-

29

mand for constitutional limitation—begin to saturate American political values: notions which reflect a reverberating fear of tyranny and a corresponding distrust of distant and concentrated authority. Along with the associated and incipient capitalism from which they derive, these values come to be generally understood as indications of a historic mission to bring a more civilized consciousness to all who inhabit the earth.

Indeed, the high era of doctrinal expression in America actually commences before natural-law philosophy congeals into a hegemonic influence, extending for more than two centuries from the earliest Puritan settlements to the end of the Civil War. During these years, an echoing concern about what ought to be and ought not to be becomes the major refrain of the American intellectual experience. This is a time of little if any significant theoretical effort with, perhaps, the exception of parts of the work of John C. Calhoun: an epoch when an a priori-deductive methodology permeates what become architectonic political constructions. It is an age when essentials are rarely questioned because what matters is assumed: including the certainty that history is on the side of the United States and that with an appropriate amount of civic will anything can be achieved. An interest in why things are as they are is seldom in evidence. It is certainly not discernible in the informing convictions upon which the American perception of revolution is predicated, and which provide the justification for an entrepreneurial ideology that cements a pluralistic system together.

Only with the trauma of the Civil War does this begin to change. Judicial review, previously implemented by the successors to the Hamiltonian faction of the Federalist party, becomes a cogent presence in America after 1865. So does the aggrandized position of the executive. Nurtured by fundamental economic commitments, what evolves is what Hamilton had thought of as the "commercial republic," that which he intended the Constitution to augment and advance: a centralization in the arrangements of political authority as they adjust to a growing collectivization of "capitalist" enterprise. This comes to typify the patent realities of a people which, since the ratification of a Madisonian Constitution, continues to assert that a vast diversity of financially interested factions is the necessary foundation of liberty.

While judicial review, despite its arcane roots in Coke and Blackstone, is truly an American contribution to the history of political institutions, its expanded authority, as the United States becomes a nation in the last quarter of the nineteenth century, actually signifies the Europeanizing of the country and of the doctrines that fortify its existence. Here is the paradoxical yield of American "nationalism," an epoch of the end of opportunity built upon the easy availability of productive land and of the arrival of the great business firm as the characteristic mode of material fabrication. It is a period in which the nation rapidly moves toward its own approximation of English and continental property relationships, with oligopoly replacing monopoly as the paramount form: a time when the distinctive quality of American political thought recedes.

What is in retreat is an order wherein the instruments of production are diverse in their ownership and control, and within which a pluralism of power and authority is the readily anticipated consequence of this presiding technological reality. As a result, with the end of the Civil War "American exceptionalism" becomes an arcane artifact—albeit, an obstinate one. Hence, as the United States moves further away from Europe in terms of years, its ideological perspective is increasingly European in content. The economic actualities of the country more closely resemble those of the Old World than they did during much of the time when America was, technically, ruled by the colonial policies of other governments.

A sense of despair becomes evident as an early response to these developments, and to a perceived conformity which the closing down of a more entrepreneurial and idyllic America

seems to impose. What is most profoundly threatened in an
industrial, and now, in a postindustrial America is the notion
of capitalist opportunity which fueled immigration into the
United States and is the raison d'être of its constitutive agreements. The constitutional component within liberalism is absorbed into the logic of an economic concentration that
dissolves its capitalist commitment.[3] It follows that the liberal
idea of revolution, which is always infused with the argument
for equal entrepreneurial opportunity and the resulting
authority of a rational meritocracy, comes to be contorted and
vague.

3. The Ideology of Entrepreneurial Residue

Despite the economic realities of the last century and a half, those who now patrol the bastions of a business civilization appear to behave as entrepreneurial stipulations instruct. This obscures our reactions to what is suspected to be an age of revolution, inducing the disorienting whispers of a strangely troubled country. Some are making it. More expect to make it. Others are pretending to make it, while the prevailing ambience is dictated by bureaucratic standards of cost accounting, and as the associated assurance that "bigger is better" becomes redundant. Public attention is accordingly consumed with admiring and emulating quantity as displayed in private material possession. All preen and fawn in deference to the "revolution" of opportunity, and elan and enthusiasm are propounded as the formal order of the day.

This is an America wherein monetary achievement loudly stipulates the worth of the self, yielding the prestige and station which are the true rewards of affluence. The exchange values of power, status, and privilege that accompany a command on money remain the premier occupation of the national existence; a presumed result of a market competition within which gratification is fleeting and "success" can never be absolute because it is invariably measured against the "success" of others; a reflection of a historic contract which insists that the enjoyment of personal accumulation must be governed by gradations of attainment and an endless obligation to possess even more.

Still, there is a growing sense that promises have been broken. Frustration abounds. The poor dream of being well-off. The well-off dream of being rich. And the rich dream of being something else as the pressure of having "arrived" often seems unbearable. The pervading sadness of the late-nineteenth century returns as a remembered melody, disrupting the customary litany of what the American Revolution was about. As always, in a time of widely perceived dislocation, a search for theory intrudes as a need to comprehend replaces a complacent certainty about what revolution actually means.

In contrast to this enervating ambivalence, there are countries that claim to welcome "revolution" and proudly affirm that they carry its banner. They applaud revolution as "progress," as the promise of improvement in a material existence that exceeds the tolerations of consent. However, a preponderance of the American people, deeply conditioned to the recollection of a "revolutionary" heritage, now confront these "alien" possibilities with an obvious trepidation and confusion of civic intention.

Of course, the Puritan influence must remain strong in a nation that could even consider defining the taking of a drink not only as illegal, but as unconstitutional. Nevertheless, in its overwhelming ramifications, the American order manifests the looming dominance of Locke. Indeed, an America which thinks of itself as unfettered by past traditions and, especially, after the Puritans, those of a feudal and dynastic politics, and which, in the European view, was once a veritable instance of the state of nature, long represents the purest systemic example of the great liberal revolution that stormed against monarchy in the Western world during the eighteenth century and which, for a magnifying portion of the planet, continues to do so in the present era. But within the ideology of liberalism lurk the seeds of a more volatile revolutionary force. Transcending the notion of an equality of rights as the opportunity for "private" wealth is the quite different claim that equality describes the very nature of the political capacity of human beings; that the logical derivation of this must be an equality of power and authority among all; and, if a majority wills it, an equality of financial condition and result.

In this manner the struggle between democracy and liberalism comes to the United States. Yet the fact is that the national substance has always expressed a duality of ideas that proceed in contradictory concurrence: ideas of crucial historical significance for all of humanity. If liberalism articulates one revolution, democracy expresses another, and it is the confluence of these two great revolutionary streams that produces the disorientation and dilemmas that incisively attend the contemporary American anxiety about a world seething with the zeal of "revolutionary" ambition.

However, the democratic advocation of progress toward the fulfillment of the telos of each through immersion in the polis actually finds the terms of its American surrender in the abiding liberal adherence to an equal opportunity to get rich: a surrender, regardless of the Jeffersonian movement and its subsequent extrapolations, which inextricably intrudes upon our understanding of what revolution and, indeed, democracy, are about. As a consequence, this becomes a land of equality which can't tolerate the realization of its own proclaimed ideals. A land of equal monetary opportunity wherein the many work hard and end up with little, and that fails to react with enthusiasm when the poor become a little less so. A land of the rational principles of natural law that avidly searches for the exuberance of the emotional and the vagaries of the philosophically Romantic. A land that admires productive work and, as a corollary, the labor "theory" of value, a formulation which is necessarily at war with a simultaneous affinity for the "rights" to, and of, property which will allegedly alleviate "scarcity" through investment at a profitable rate of return. A land that deeply despises government while striving to impose replications of its own government on a global scale.[1] A land wherein an apparent hypocrisy is the prevailing theme of its economic, social, and political existence: a land that actually knows itself not at all and which, therefore, is always surprised about what is abundantly predictable.

A land that historically stands for revolution which currently emerges as the power center of counterrevolution in a postindustrial world.

Failing to apprehend our own history, we attempt to dance
in place while eagerly acclaiming the integral motion of it all.
The tendency toward wealth concentration and an endemic
economic depression—which is the logical result of the invisible hand—becomes more extreme, and the search for a national agenda insistently gravitates to a previous and
"preferable" era that the preponderance of the population
knows nothing of now, and knew nothing of then. Despite the
theory of diminishing marginal utility, and its clarification of
the fact that the desire for additional wealth generally becomes less intense as personal affluence and a sense of financial security grows, a preoccupation with the arrival of a newly
rediscovered "scarcity"—the harvest of federal and corporate
policy for the past two decades, and more—allows no entertainment of the thought that material deprivation may not be
required. Oblivious to any knowledge of the corporatism
within our actual tradition—or of the ramifying intensity of
technocratic interests—we welcome the "return" of an entrepreneurial nation to the normalcy of "the opportunity society."

But such is the story of our experience. Almost without exception, every important "reform" effort in American history
tries to recover an earlier, and entrepreneurial, time, and
what is considered "progressive" is a dimly perceived prior
epoch which is portrayed as a superior configuration of human relationships. With the exception of the labor movement
and, importantly, of the enterprise of science, the status-quo
ante is invariably the goal of social change in a "revolutionary"
America. Hence the nation once again reaches for the great-
ness of its past with little concern about what that past actually
meant for enormous aggregates of people scratching for sub-
sistence on southern and western farms or in the sweatshops
of cities; not to mention those held as slaves and the subjec-
tion of Native Americans to a policy of extermination for more
than a century; a time now celebrated as an era of "liberty"
which—as usual—is in the process of "decline."

Only recently is even a hint of this tacitly acknowledged. The immediate situation bears witness to the corrosive influence of the end of ideology, to the exhaustion of ideas. But what is really exhausted is the historical American affection for the ethos of revolution. The mandated certainty of America as revolution is replaced by an equal assurance that all revolutions conclude where they start—or that they simply make matters worse—giving credence to the Platonic notion that revolution must result in the enervation and anomie which has to follow the expenditure of misdirected idealism in the quest of futility.

Accordingly, scholars, and other guardians of tradition, remind any who will listen about the wisdom of classical form; of the associated fact that revolution really means to go around; that, despite momentary delusions about turning the tables, the Thermidor and the Restoration can't be avoided; and that the misdirected energy which fuels what parades as advance can only result in the impressive systemic cost which presages an inevitable return to an anterior condition. Some of the recent tyrants reemerge while those who were tyrannized before often become tyrants themselves. Such an outcome, as Plato insisted, is the absolute consequence of the nature of man: a necessity which leads to the conviction that the stability of the Republic is far better than the chaos and human devastation which must attend any attempt to transform what exists into more than can be achieved.

A people devoid of any controlling vision other than an elitist liberalism—which confines "progress" to gross domestic product—takes the admonition of Plato very seriously. To preserve the civility of the republic against a globe rampant with revolution becomes a salient preoccupation of its dominant policy: a policy which searches for a semblance of "reason" within what towers up as a chaotic world.

It is within this ideological vortex that America becomes extant proof that the idea of revolution as human progress, an idea which inspires the liberal beginning, was really a mis-

guided adventure that is finally being corrected. Not surprisingly, we look in the only possible direction, a myopic glimpse
into the golden age of a presumed past that never was, yet, as
depicted by those who speak for the national will, which exemplifies what must be restored. Reflexively committed to the
pervasive liberal formulation of equal commercial opportunity, the United States becomes a nation of revolution which
loses its revolutionary elan and—in its most essential expression—all assumable purpose.

We thus become the inhabitants of a century when progress
abruptly stops and when the most relevant question of the age
is at what point we went wrong. Our dreams are of the glories
of old while the emergent is perceived opaquely and with
dread, and with an inflexible knowledge that it threatens
those established proprieties which compose the guiding values of any worthwhile civilization. Exceeding even the popularizers, those who ascend to the mantle of specialized
political intelligence give voice to this perception. Rarely being members of the class they aspire to, they associate themselves with the status and privilege that this class can bestow.
They become sycophants to entrenched power, mandarins
who learnedly inform us that progress, in the sense of the
authentic improvement of human beings, ended about a century ago; that the multiplication of gadgetry and material technique is the totality of what is conceivable; and, for a ramifying
dimension of the social wisdom, is all that ever was conceivable in the first place.

Still, a disturbing absence of coherence typifies the intrusive
discord of such a retreat. Perhaps America has not had time to
smooth off the rough edges of its ideological tensions and
become known to itself. Or the reasons may be otherwise.
Indeed, in a day-to-day sense, the reasons do not appear to
matter—although they actually do. We who search for our
generational meaning are part of the continuum of history
and, not knowing this, we become absorbed into a culture that
can't appraise its own causalities and, thereby, its own being.

Nonetheless, we grudgingly discover that memory intrinsically demands more than the relentless cacophony of a current-events perspective. And we must deal with this. But to act we must know, and the desire to ascertain the process of historical change becomes a pressing—if obscurely recognized—need.

Yet little of this is consciously understood by most of us, and clearly not by the great waves of human beings that invade this country in the late-nineteenth and early-twentieth centuries, and that now invade from other parts of the globe. These are people who—notwithstanding a nostalgia for their ethnic and national backgrounds—labor with diligence and, at times, desperation, to achieve an identity that will transform them into "Americans." And such is an identity that pointedly attempts to realize itself in the revolution of entrepreneurial opportunity; a preeminent ethos that suppresses the socialist priorities that also emigrate from Europe; an ethos, however, which plainly eludes any translation into reality as the twentieth century proceeds. Those who arrive in the United States seeking the free-market realities of a liberal consciousness are incessantly confronted by the bureaucratic imperatives of corporate enterprise, and by their subtle insinuation into the authority and policies of the state.

All of this makes for a confused and jingoistic population which is busy repeating comforting stories about market opportunities told in the parlance of a constitutionally protected individualism. These become truths which presently impose an ambience of uncertainty on a land wherein the assurance that motion takes place only within the distorted recollections of an outmoded economic form is an ideological requirement. And such is an uncertainty that finally challenges the presumption that revolution, or even significant systemic transition, is compatible with the fundamental character of the nation.

Of course, we are told—by those who will admit it—that this

is to be expected. The United States, it is propounded, is a "nation of immigrants"; a melting pot of nationalities or, more precisely, a stew, wherein myriad ingredients maintain much of their original shape and flavor; too recently a part of the recipe to be certain of themselves as sufficiently homogenized into a people with a shared history. Still, the strange truth is that those who are here the longest are the most puzzled about what it means to be an American. It is the more-recently arrived, and their children, who are the most vociferous "patriots," providing support for a persistent chorus of nationalistic superiority which is translated into a counterrevolutionary interpretation of "Americanism" by the media.

Here is the culmination of truth through advertising: a country of great ethnic and national complexity and geographic size wherein dwell those who specialize in the instant expertise of the glib and the facile. These propagate the illusion of American diversity; a proposal held together by a revolutionary vision of market opportunities which actually denies the gestalt of community by formulating society as nothing more than the sum total of the discrete entities that comprise it; a revolution which opposes the "Marxist" revolutions that not long ago appeared to be relentless in their encroachment upon the century. Literally an exercise in nation building, such pronouncements are enhanced by a technocratic espousal of the "facts" which cogently signifies the "information society."

Nonetheless, the notion that the United States as a melting pot represents a revolutionary experiment in the affairs of mankind misses the essential point because it misses the essential reality. The American experiment is revolutionary only because we are subsumed into an essential and entrepreneurial liberalism: an ideological reflex which is the central variable of an order that constitutes the most extreme manifestation of one of the major revolutions in human history. And it is explicitly this revolution which is now under assault by more expansive revolutionary aspirations.

If, as has been recently "discovered"—once again—a successful claim to knowledge is power, what is accepted as knowledge must accord with the consciousness of those who listen as well as of those who expound. Augmented by the commercial elitism which accompanies the paramount liberal conception of equal rights, and driven by the idea of a perennial scarcity of wealth within a world populated by materially insatiable beings, "knowledge" of the natural laws of economics leads to a persistent and frenetic activity in pursuit of personal monetary gain, an activity which wears people out, leaving them depleted, alienated, and devoid of larger societal goals. Accordingly, the many worry about financial survival as they clash over "social issues" while the technocracy governs: a stratum of power and authority that respects no doctrinal line between the "private" and the "public," or the "economic" and the "political." Supporting this, all efforts toward a more egalitarian distribution of power and authority are effectively frustrated by the reflexive appeal of a red-scare which finds its seeds in the Puritan foundations of the national experience, and which becomes an even more active participant in the national mentality since the Bolshevik Revolution.

However, in an America that now reaches for meaning and direction the pretense can't hold. The United States must finally confront the realty that the issue of revolution is the centerpiece of its history. And it must deal with the dilemmas of power which emanate from the fact that as entrepreneurial opportunity is melded into the technocratic concerns of a planetary mercantilism its commitment to revolution closes down.

Thus, at the height of its empire, American liberalism is curiously tired, unsure of its bearing, its proponents, as always, struggling for a sense of who they really are. The ideological supremacy of private monetary ambition renders the population less "political" while a yearning for a pluralistic equilibrium infuses the substance of its will. There is in America a melancholy earlier suggested by Tocqueville, and by the sub-

sequent quest of Emerson and Thoreau to transcend the dislo-
cations of industrial development: a melancholy that attests to
the static quality of a nation getting old before its time. Perhaps it isn't astonishing that a country so new is a country so
stratified: a country wherein, by 1962, the top one-half of one
percent owned and managed more money than the bottom
eighty-one percent of the population;[2] or, put another way,
wherein, by 1986, 1.6 percent of the population had holdings
amounting to more than the total gross national product of
that same year;[3] and wherein the dream of equal power is
eradicated by an admiration for a corporatist control of an
incredibly bloated proportion of the productive wealth.[4] A
country wherein income distributions become increasingly
more typical of third-world economic systems than those of its
Western European counterparts.

Go around again. This time you might get the brass ring.

Or at least your kids might.

4. Liberty, Freedom, and Revolution

Having attained the goals of the first stage of nationalism—
that which consolidates a people with a common language
and customs into a viable nation-state—the United States em-
barks upon the second stage of the nationalist adventure, that
which turns us into the great purveyor of "progress" and "revolution" to the globe. Such a disposition is patently incipient in
the early years of the republic. Deep within the historical consciousness of America resides the certainty of an anointed role
as a rational model for all humanity: a conviction which becomes aggressive in the nineteenth-century obligations of
manifest destiny and in the twentieth-century need to save the
world for "democracy."

Still, as Tocqueville suggests, a liberal population, innocent
of medieval and dynastic traditions, may be incapable of ap-
preciating the struggles of others for the same liberties it en-
joys. This becomes a cogent observation about the American
perception of revolution. Within this context, of course, "liberty" refers to the expansion of the franchise as well as to due
process of law, areas in which the United States was more
egalitarian than the regimes of continental Europe at that
time. Because of the frontier character of the agrarian south
and west, which led to a broad-scale ownership of productive
land and a resulting qualification to vote, even England in the
early-nineteenth century had not reached the American
achievement.

As a consequence, few countries then applauded the political, social, and economic equality that America told itself it
represented. Yet the proposition that material avarice works
for the betterment of the nation and, by extension, the entire
earth, an idea drawn from the doctrinal arguments of the
early proponents of capitalism, leads to the most vital contradiction within the present situation: a contradiction which en-

genders those obtuse proclamations that array liberty against equality and individualism against mutuality. These are tensions that permeate our history, deriving from values, attitudes, and perceptions which date, at least, from the last quarter of the eighteenth century.

Here is found a central uncertainty within the American people about who they are and with what voice they speak to themselves and to others. If the immediate intention of politics is the formulation and implementation of public policy, the effort to influence contemporary policy is a continuation of that dialectical unity of the partisans of Hamilton as opposed to those of Jefferson: of the prerogatives and presumed social worth and governing capacity of persons of private wealth in contrast to the promise of equality as something more than an unlikely opportunity to become one of the wealthy few. But this discord of opposites within the national consciousness, which is finally an argument about the meaning of revolution, is rarely detected because of a fixation which holds that the stability of the United States is already grounded in political equality, and that the only real issue is the distribution of income—and not of power and authority.

Despite this, however, America is now in reaction against a profound revolutionary development which demands a far more egalitarian comprehension of power and human worth. What this testifies to is a habitual inability to confront democracy as an essential aspiration that assails all special claims to political authority throughout the experience of the species. It reveals an ideological circumvention of the fact that much of the occupation of governing classes—and of the political elites within them—is to mollify this aspiration while maintaining their own ruling positions. It is to ignore the point that meaningful community is always a matter of shared power, not of rights, not even of property rights. But to be myopic about this is exactly symptomatic of the success of a liberalism that denigrates politics and promotes economics as an equal opportunity for people to demonstrate how unequal they really are.[1] It

is what America is in those periods when it denies the Jeffersonian constituent of its own tradition: periods which typify
the national existence most of the time.

Plainly, the United States is seen by multitudes throughout
the globe as the greatest purveyor of counterrevolution in the
present era. Such is a judgment which discloses a central paradox within the very stuff of American politics: a paradox that
becomes more pronounced in the twentieth century as the
scope of our involvements becomes more imperialistic, but
which actually epitomizes the understanding of revolution
that infuses our history. For more than two-hundred years,
America could congratulate itself for being the vanguard of
the liberal revolution in an age of extant and evolving nation-
states: and it continues to do so. Yet it concurrently opposes a
further revolution which ramifies from the predilections of
people whom the proponents of liberal opportunity never intended to include—and who begin to apply its notions of
equal rights to themselves. And, because rights have no meaning without the ability to implement them, this ultimately becomes the doctrinal basis of the democratic advocation for an
equality of power and political authority—and even of condition and result. It is this movement from equal rights and
equal opportunity to equal freedom—from economics to
power—that the United States now confronts and resists. This
is to be expected. Democracy must incite a subversion of the
presiding elitism of the liberal order: an order which reacts by
becoming "conservative" while continuing to assert that it is
the only legitimate version of revolution as a historic force.

It follows that those who populate this most stable of political systems also are convinced they are the most "revolutionary" people in human history. The deep strain of anarchy
within the liberal idea impels them toward the "private" and
an avoidance of the "public," offering the soothing illusion of
control, at least in regard to more immediately ascertained
monetary interests—even as the greater world insistently im-

pinges upon such "personal" considerations. When organized
into groups, these preoccupations become the commercial
core of American pluralism. But to be "pluralistic" in this
sense is to resemble animals that merely collect their environment instead of human beings who create it. It is to live within
the distorted and alienated confinement of Plato's cave, sure
that the shadows are reality. It is to deny what is unique to
humanity and implicit in its attempt to achieve dignity and
recognition; the need for polis; for civic effect: a need which
incessantly seeks greater articulation as concerns about financial security, despite all official efforts to the contrary, become
steadily less overwhelming and pervasive.

Although their perceptions of the proper delegations of political authority were "conceived in liberty," the inhabitants of
British North America did not actually engage in a revolution
against established principles. What they were involved in was
a coup d'etat or, at most, "a justified rebellion,"[2] that might
ensure their "rights as Englishmen." Yet the War of Independence actually contained a far more revolutionary impulse
which was suppressed during the battle for release from the
suzerainty of Whitehall, an impulse which found later actualization in Shays' Rebellion and in the magnitude of the Jeffersonian movement. Thus expressed was an egalitarian particle
within the market elitism of a dominant liberal consciousness,
and those who advanced this contradiction in regard to the
several British colonies—as well as to the later revolution in
France—were usually suspected of being unduly influenced by
"alien ideas"—a penchant for dismissal which congeals into a
national habit.

Here was a movement, however, that could successfully challenge the "right" to chattel property in the Northwest Ordi-
nances. It is a movement which today continues to
counterpose a contention for opportunity as power and
authority against the cramped liberal view of opportunity as
money. In so doing, it is classically democratic: lauding not

property rights and individual wealth aggrandizement, but the historical search for those connections which link power, actualization, and freedom into a more genuinely human environment. "Men like John Adams and Washington were not attempting to overturn our social and economic system, but rather to set the English North American colonies up as an independent nation-state." Nevertheless, "it is a rare territorial-nationalist revolution that is purely territorial, purely nationalist. Sam Adams, Tom Paine, Jefferson himself, were trying to do more than just cut us off from the British Crown; they were trying to make us a more perfect society according to the ideals of the Enlightenment."[3]

In the end, this generates a confused national identity, an ideological condition which devolves from a failure to perceive that revolution must finally be constructed upon a distinction between liberty and freedom.[4] As Arendt argues the point, once people are beyond the "necessity" which infuses material deprivation, "the end of rebellion is liberation, while the end of revolution is the foundation of freedom": a foundation that becomes manifest in the fact that "political freedom, generally speaking, means the right 'to be a participator in government,' or it means nothing."[5] There is, then, a pivotal difference between liberty from and freedom to, and if the "revolution" against England augmented the general liberty of individuals and populations in the several ex-colonies, it did little to redefine and expand the distribution of the power and authority necessary to the civic action inferred by freedom.

To replace personnel with "better" people is reform or, at most, a putsch or a coup d'etat; to increase liberty from the authority of the state is a rebellion. While the American "Revolution" did mitigate tyranny in the name of rights, its principal outcome, despite the objections of American democrats, was to leave the ongoing arrangements of power and authority— and the values and attitudes that these arrangements reflected—alone. Certainly, the controlling assumption behind the conception of the pursuit of happiness, "whether Jefferson knew it or not, was that no one could be called happy without his share in public happiness, that no one could be called free without his experience in public freedom, and that no one could be called either happy or free without participating, and having a share, in public power."[6] But the pursuit of happiness, as Jefferson conceived it, was never a war aim of most of those who directed the political and military conflict of the mid-1770s and the early 1780s, and even liberty was essentially promoted in the afterthought of a Bill of Rights which most of the dominant Federalists accepted only because the authority delegations of their Constitution couldn't be ratified without it.

This reigning American failure to confront the crucial gulf between liberty as the absence of "natural" or "artificial" restraint, and freedom as public action, leads to a politics which renders "revolution" opaque. It currently assures those who don't rule that they actually do[7] by transforming liberalism into "democracy": a distinction that those who fought the battle against England had no illusions about. The American colonists were predominantly republicans, not democrats: financial and rational elitists, not champions of political equality. Hence "the republican form of government recommended itself to the pre-revolutionary political thinkers not because of its egalitarian character (the confusing and confused equation of republican with democratic government dates from the nineteenth century) but because of its promise of great durability,"[8] a durability that stood in contrast to the turbulence both of monarchy and democratic rule. It was this which Jefferson referred to as "a republican, or popular government, of the second grade of purity";[9] clearly not the democracy of the ward republic; but preferable to more absolutist configurations of political authority.

The influence of an earlier Lockian ideology ensured that the liberal vision of a pluralized distribution of power and authority among members of an entrepreneurial elite preceded the War of Independence; that the war was between liberal systems at varying points of development; and that the outcome was that a more atomized liberal constitution replaced a more centralized one. Indeed, except as a further instance of a revolutionary liberalism which was sweeping the Western world, the American Revolution was not a revolution at all. It was a rebellion that would eventually bring forth a nation, within which the primary issue was the promise of financial opportunity that infused an already-existing British liberalism and which had previously achieved ideological credence through the increasingly accepted assumptions of natural law and natural rights.

Accordingly, within the domains of power, authority, and privilege, the struggle against English liberalism yields a liberal result, replete with that combination of elitism and a distrust of human nature which characterizes constitutional government: as well as with a system of entrepreneurial competition which will signify who the members of "The Aristocracy of Wealth and Talents"[10] truly are.

Such is a view of revolution that Americans are comfortable with and, in moments of perceived dislocation, to which they reflexively return. Led by the cheerleaders of an unrestrained free enterprise, most people find a right to commercial profitability to be the only depiction of revolution at all worthy of approval. The Jeffersonian proposal of power as human opportunity and the road to the public happiness is twisted into a bourgeois neutralization of power through capitalist competition: a formulation wherein the right kind of economics—including a corporate economics—dictates the very definition of a civilized existence. Within the abiding necessities that America sets for itself, the pursuit of happiness becomes the "market," producing little happiness even as it acclaims unremitting pursuit.

This bit of ideological doublethink which comprises "liberal-democracy"—an extrapolation of British developments in the seventeenth century—remains in charge of our conception of revolution at the very moment that liberalism reaches outside of the West to much of the world. American policy must deal with this in the international arena, striving to reconcile a corporatist imperialism with the pressures of this intrusion while sufficiently deferring to our traditional claim that all who become party to the obligations of the Lockian contract are instantly entitled to a civic clarification and protection of their natural rights. But the United States must also contend with more expansive revolutionary rumblings at home. What this comes down to is the application of equal opportunity to power and authority as well as to economics: the unsettling effect of a Jeffersonian predilection which now intrudes upon the supremacy of liberal perceptions, confounding the national commitment to revolution and, as a result, the prevailing focus of contemporary politics.

Still, as long as the great generality of Americans can't discern the conclusive distinction between liberty and freedom, as well as the necessary connectedness of freedom to power, our ambivalence about a revolutionary age will remain a pervading discord of the order. Or, more precisely, it will acutely express the process of the liberal revolution engaging in historical resistance to one which is democratic.

Without actually knowing it, and within the limits of our conformity, these are the forces that the generation of the 1950s was attempting to grasp.

5. The "Explosion" of the Nineteen-Sixties

"Although the masters make the rules of the wise men and the fools I got nothing, ma, to live up to."[1] Suddenly a strident call; although not really suddenly. The song of the sixties was truly ours of the fifties. But our voice failed. Silenced and contorted by the fear of Communism, or of being assailed as its agent, we lacked the ability to sing in a way that could be heard. We shared the dream of democracy. Yet we were tired, worn out before our time, before we even began, as a repressed rage which can't find outlet invariably appears as unbearable fatigue, and will do so, until it bursts into the open, as somber clouds move past the sun, much to the shock of those who have learned to find solace in the dark. Thus did we of the fifties finally reveal ourselves in the sixties. The silent generation, we would put our brand on the sixties; a brand which is unacknowledged; a brand that gives to our generation a meaning in the story of America which we still fail to perceive because it is only through our displaced anger that we understand our own role.

The object of this anger, in myriad disguised forms, was that which for us epitomized official America; a hidden imperialism beyond the legal boundaries of the nation and within; a lack of "relevance" other than the making of more money. Still, disturbed as we were about our present, our history, and the lies told about each, our feelings were never discerned by others—or by ourselves. We were the compliant, anxious to conform so as to enter those circles of professional, financial, and social opportunity which we so deeply abhorred and so ardently desired.

Only through an awareness of our generational angst, muted by the presence of the Soviet reality and Western and liberal reactions to it, can we attempt to discover the revolutionary essence which is the salient political reality of our time.

In such a quest, we may come to realize that historical commonalities render absurd the preoccupations of our generational perspective, that what seems unique to us may be the same for all. Even so, it is only through the glass of this perspective that we can at least darkly glimpse the commonalities. Only through the references of our own lives can we make sense of a larger human experience and incorporate it into our conscious existence. What we must do is battle our generational myopia by accepting the fact that the search for political truth transcends generations and is ultimately an enterprise of continually magnifying dimensions.

A seizure of political authority is a specific and identifiable event. But it isn't a revolution because revolutions aren't made by revolutionaries. And they can't be made by one generation. We of the fifties really did what we had to do; seize enough power to make it possible for the music of the sixties to be heard; according it an opportunity that none would accord to us. We are, indeed, the silent generation. Yet we are also a generation of silent subversion. If our part in the unfolding of change isn't recognized, that is finally because we fail to recognize ourselves.

Not comprehending our own generation, we can't place ourselves within the larger contours of history. However, only by confronting the one can we attempt to appraise the other. Only then can we begin to evaluate our generational position, and how we fit into the greater scheme of those persistent needs which motivate the sequence of ideas and events that express the realities of human power and which animate what is known as the revolutionary process.

The explosion of the 1960s deeply shocked those of us who were nurtured on the red-scare. It was—and still is—difficult for members of our generation to conceive that the political reflexes of the United States aren't generically repressive, anxious to silence any who dare to object to a national mission to impose the "private" control of material production upon the entire planet. Hence it was almost impossible for us to believe that the McCarthyite country we knew so well had become a place that we didn't know at all.

Perhaps if we had thought a little about the dialectics of social movements we would have been less startled. We might have remembered that Lenin failed to finish *State and Revolution*—in which he forecast that any significant change in Russia was fifty years away at the earliest—because he had to "lead" a revolution that was "abruptly" breaking out;[2] and we may have better ascertained that throughout human history "the people move eternally in the elements of surprise."[3] Nevertheless, we welcomed the sixties, and did what we could do, while trying to identify with those of a later generation who didn't appear to share our concerns about articulating their criticisms in an overtly public manner.

So the resonance of the egalitarian chorus grew louder. As did the accompanying Jeffersonian lyrics that had somehow found a voice that could now be heard—and to which some were apparently listening. Phrased in the nomenclature of "participatory democracy," these were lyrics that sounded familiar. After all, we had practiced them much—albeit quietly. We were aware that "rights" had evolved into a subterfuge for the power of concentrated property claims and, if not for fascism as a Romantic nationalism, at least for its liberal variation which, in ensuing years, would be labeled as a kind of "friendly fascism."[4] Some even conjectured, however obliquely, that Jefferson was finally an advocate of power, not of rights, and especially not a right to accumulate more property than what was required for a reasonable level of material comfort, a right which couldn't be allowed to impede the historical gravitation toward a greater equality of influence in civic affairs: that all property claims must conclusively give way if they intruded upon "the fundamental right to labour the earth"[5] simply because control of at least a piece of the instruments of production is always necessary to political equality.

A few of us might even have suspected that his initial resistance to the Constitution was based exactly on this. We sensed what Jefferson well knew, that the decency and individual independence activated through affiliation with the polis were feasible only to the extent that power and authority were equal and that, in a country that centrally valued private wealth, the distribution of property was critical to the kind of distribution of freedom and power that could serve the principle of majority rule.

But what we were opaque about was that majority rule has little to do with mass voting and plebescites—that the argument for small, self-governing ward republics was merely a vehicle which might stimulate the further development of the civilizing impulses within the human personality. It was, nevertheless, plain, as Alan Wolfe would afterward put it,[6] that the desire for meaningful community is an indelible aspiration that won't disappear, no matter how often betrayed by the distant manipulations of false leaders and the corollary gullibilities of vast elements of large populations. Yet, within the day-to-day maelstrom that informed the decade, we were slow to realize that the call for "relevance" and a ramifying counterculture were manifestations of a classical democratic demand for a greater equality of public authority. Looking for leadership, we couldn't understand that a strong leader makes a weak people, that "a strong people is the only lasting strength,"[7] and disgusted with the support of regressive policies by much of organized labor, we ignored the fact that the complementary association between self-government and the need for work as an outward expression of the inner person said something fundamental about the inherent substance of revolution.

6. The Rational Core of the Nineteen-Sixties

The current attempt to disparage the ultimate rationality of the resistance to official policy, foreign and domestic, in the 1960s is really an effort to portray such resistance as subversive of the national character. It follows that the activities of those years become the intrigues of an "alien" force, in all probability the work of dupes, if not the willing agents, of what was then the Soviet Union. Or, more mildly, they are depicted as an instance of a "creedal passion" that articulates the "egalitarian" foundation of the American consciousness: a periodic surge of moralism which, along with cynicism, complacency, and hypocrisy, constitutes the anticipated patterns of a tradition exemplified by a great deal of illusory motion even as it guarantees that nothing important can change.[1] Beyond this, in more "sophisticated" circles, the movement of the 1960s is found to be a Romantic critique of Rationalism, the hurling of misguided emotion against a civilization established upon the expectation of the historical primacy of reason.

In a special way, some of these charges are true. After all, what the United States finds rational is *The Wall Street Journal* plausibly introducing itself as "The Daily Diary of the American Dream." And this isn't surprising in a nation ideologically imbued with the market values of the capitalist perception: a perception that applauds natural law while endorsing an order which devours nature by transforming the earth into commodities[2] as it simultaneously reassures its devotees that the human appetite for ever-larger quantities of exchange value is insatiable. To be poor and to believe this, to become the alienated creature that is commodity man, is understandable. But where abundance is at least within reach, to pursue lucre with an unmitigated societal intensity is to act out a consciousness that feeds off scarcity and plainly can't tolerate the threat of material sufficiency. Of course, where private wealth accords the privilege and recognition that flows from status and power an endless need for monetary acquisition might be considered reasonable. Yet, even here, "rational economic man" virtually becomes opposed to reason if reason is comprehended as that which advances the literal survival of a species that requires a supportive environment in order to thrive.

But, then, there is tradition. And tradition is our most important product. So much so that we invent a fresh batch of it every day. Nonetheless, the economy isn't exactly static and things do actually change as the distributive and dialectical logic of "capitalism" proceeds toward concentration, and as the disquieting pressures of a glimpsed affluence begin to intrude. The integrity of the order must be maintained and—at least since the days of bread and circuses—entertainment is the prescribed cohesive, offering populations diversion as an escape from the grim probabilities of their material situation.

In an epoch of overwhelming technological productivity, this urgent function becomes more complex. Entertainment not only salves the desperation of the poor; it now becomes a crucial element of meaning for the well-off in a land which typically has no clue as to how to cope with leisure. Show business replaces leisure with recreation, thus assuring that boredom doesn't translate into a democratic immersion into the polis and, as a result, actual citizenship. Where the self-motivation of activating stimuli isn't awarded much credence the need for simple stimuli becomes extreme precisely because they are so transitory, and because their central manifestation in a voracious consumerism[3] is not really likely for all—or, indeed, for too many—in a corporatist America which stipulates that most people must have less so that sufficient wealth acquisition can find its intended exchange value in recognition, status, and privilege. To protect the ideological commitment to "equal opportunity" and, thereby, the accepted configurations of power and authority, poverty—both absolute and relative—remains vital. Still, the many have to be assuaged, and a neoclassical emphasis on production becomes notably fused with entertainment and celebrity, while those who comprise this pivotal industry are paid in reference to their societal as well as their commercial worth.

Where this leads us is not surprising. We come to inhabit a country wherein the residue of capitalism is best represented by an advertising culture which can seriously project Disneyland as a major contribution to human progress. In this manner we traverse the distance from "Monopoly" to Mickey Mouse. Or to "The Breakfast of Champions." Or, maybe more appropriately, to an addiction to Goofy. Exciting possibilities for the "rationalism" of those now so eager to denigrate the 1960s.

In fact, the 1960s expressed an interior struggle within an America that wants to associate its experience with the egalitarian ambience of the Declaration of Independence while also adhering to the United States Constitution as reported out of Philadelphia—a document, without certain of its amendments, that is primarily concerned with capital accumulation and the promotion and protection of private investment through ensuring the control of productive property by competing financial elites. Accordingly, what the sixties most profoundly witnessed was an assault by a Jeffersonian rationalism against the Madisonian reason of the Constitution, as well as against a Hamiltonian raison d'être which provides the ideological justification for the corporatist system that America has become. It is this assault upon itself which centrally infused a decade wherein the egalitarian predilection within the duality of the American revolutionary tradition emerged as evident once again.

That the upheavals of the 1960s set much of the subsequent national agenda by moving the country toward an expanded equality of legal rights, a focus on the environment, and a reflexive suspicion of governmental justifications for war—"constitutional" or otherwise—is patent enough. So is the fact that their impact was more global and historical than is often surmised. "Prior to the New Left, there was a widespread belief that industrialized societies were harmonious social systems which, internally at least, contained no major oppositional forces."[4] This was even more true of postindustrial orders wherein the countervailing power of labor unions is absorbed into the planning operations of those multinational corporations which articulate and sell the values and attitudes that yield the presiding realities of public policy. Throughout the Western world, the conviction that the stability of government was furthered by a constellation of technical and monetary expertise was proclaimed as "the end of ideology": a conviction which was abruptly challenged by events that induced a pervading concern about the legitimacy of "the system" and the propriety of business influence—a challenge that is yet to cease.

However, and especially in the United States, those involved in the turmoil of the sixties were obtuse in exactly that arena wherein political theory matters most. We didn't directly confront the issue of power because, unlike that of Jefferson, our outlook was devoid of a philosophical materialism[5] and, consequently, of any economic and technological analysis. The real deficiency of the movement of that time was not that it failed to publicize elitism and privilege in an "egalitarian" America, but that it didn't get at the actual basis of the salient values and attitudes that blend the population into a coherent political order. And it is exactly these values and attitudes which eventuate in a consciousness that releases the incessant amplification of market power and its monopolistic and oligopolistic capture of the basic industries—among others—a condition which becomes rampant in the vertical integration and the conglomerate and concentric formations that finance the esteemed "professionalism" of technobureaucratic authority.

Not that power was ignored; clearly, the 1960s were an overt reaction to power which was perceived as dominant and even tyrannical. Yet the epoch couldn't deal with the questions of why power existed in the manner that it did; of what created its particular organization and content; and, most specifically, of the necessity of such power within the operative imperatives of research and development that fuel modern production. This is because we didn't trace power to its roots: to the understanding that the privilege and status we claimed to detest were not simply reflections of big money but, more deeply, were the opposite faces of the very texture of power. In this we were myopic about the fact that democracy is far more than a majoritarian process and its policy results: that democracy mandates a revolutionary view of economics, and of its connections to human fulfillment and to the kind of power and authority which might allow political equality to move toward its actualization.

Inherent within the doctrine of democracy is hidden a more expansive revolution now disguised by the scientific and technological sources of contemporary power. This speaks to what is universal about the human experience: the insistent articulation of the ambitions and fears of the species propounded at a civic and discernible level. Revolution isn't an occasional upheaval which America happens to presently resist. It is, instead, the stubborn expression of aspiration, brought into being by those who are seen so "seldom as . . . a cauldron and a reservoir of the human reserves that shape history."[6] Such is an expression that far exceeds the narrow notion of opportunity which permeates the politics of the country. Becoming vocalized in the 1960s as a call for "relevance," it defines opportunity as action in the public space, demanding the egalitarian quality of democratic behavior, and of labor power that is not alienated from those who work. In short, it announces the classical idea of citizenship—but for all, not only a few— along with the corollary opportunity to become human through labor in a fuller and more gratifying sense.

Notwithstanding all, or any, of this, it is the liberal idea of opportunity as commerce which continues to control any favorable reception to "revolution" in the United States. The exceptions are transposed into aberrations. Hence the 1960s are turned into a Romantic rejection of reason and the infantilism of spoiled brats, a rendition which is "proven" by ceaseless repetition and the well-publicized behavior of some of the "leaders" of that decade who come to espouse the status-quo ante for their own monetary and, at times, political advantage. This stress on personality and events as opposed to history and process, intrinsic in the drama-seeking technology of mass communication, is hyped as reality in an order wherein the messages of media are truth and wherein truth, so derived, becomes "public opinion" or, more accurately, a volatile and ever-changing public fascination. By casting light on the faddish periphery of a resistance that directed itself to civil rights, a military adventure in Asia, and the issues of environment, history is rewritten in an effort to neutralize it. Those who understand rational behavior as rule by Mickey Mouse are accordingly determined to paint the 1960s as an era when an absence of reason was loosed: a time when a transient discord in the natural harmony of the nation prevailed.

7. "Liberal Opportunity" in a Corporatist America

The dream of America is always an immigrant's dream. Its success is a tribute to the allure of the revolutionary power of the liberal idea. Each generation buys into the supposition that this is the land of equal opportunity, seldom noticing that "opportunity" is invariably subject to the hegemony of a corporatist technocracy, and that privilege derived from the proper position in the social hierarchy is a more ineffable element of American life than most are able to admit. Whether conceived of as classes or elites, competing, in gradation, or otherwise— or as some combination of each—and whether the issue is domestic or a matter of the "national interest" as this becomes central to an increasingly dominant foreign policy, these are the controlling constituents of the order. A media-pronounced "truth" may acclaim the political diversity of a people who don't quite know who they are. Yet the ingredients of power belie the alleged pluralism of a country that applauds differences of region and style even as it cheers on the force which assiduously absorbs the vast range of individual financial opportunity into the concentrated authority of technobureaucratic rule.

This discloses something supremely important about a collection of nationalities striving to become a nation. Transcending and, in fact, revealed by personal wealth accumulation, the premier enterprise of America is always an abiding search for identity. But this is constrained by our view of history and, most cogently, of revolution, as written by those in power: a view which emanates from a selection of "data" which are melded into the "core values" of a people and, perhaps more critically, by data which are lost because they find no place in the conventional perspective.

In America, as elsewhere, every revolution isn't loved quite the same.

From the depths of the thermidoric reaction to the 1960s we must realize that our experience involves two revolutions; that even the war that severs the colonies in North America from the authority of London camouflages a parallel movement to change the substance and delegations of power, property, and privilege within the emerging states; and that the defeat of this effort is pivotal to how Americans learn to visualize the formative patterns of their own tradition. Thus, within the domain of "revolution," the connotation intrudes. However, the denotation is notoriously murky, while the certainty that this is a revolutionary age seizes the operative premises of American politics. Regardless of a growing suspicion that the United States increasingly betrays its own revolutionary ideals, for millions of human beings throughout the planet, as well as for its own population, including most who consider themselves to be "conservatives," America still signifies the cutting edge of revolution: the hope of liberty and, ultimately, freedom, that revolution infers since the Enlightenment. Nonetheless, those who should know warn the nation that revolutionary zeal is currently running wild and demands cautious evaluation. Indeed, the need to be alert to the dangers of revolution as a fundamental global threat now ramifies as an indispensable test of political literacy.

Yet, also nurtured on a Jeffersonian conception of revolution as progress—as a linear movement toward a greater equality of financial result which allows a fuller opportunity for each to discover and develop the best within themselves—many find the popularity of a cramped and static rendition of the human possibilities disorienting—the bustle of animal activity within an aimless and futile milieu. Oblivious to the connection between the search for the inner self to legal power—and, more concretely, to those material sources of such power which render it ideologically acceptable—what we

apprehend is a frozen immediacy busily attempting to replicate an opaquely understood past—even as the glib utterances
of technocratic authority confirm the preferred position and
social goals of those who effectively own the country.

The long run, as John Maynard Keynes reminds us, matters
little to those who must cope with the present. But without the
long run there can be no useful systemic or personal perception. Hence, in a country that knows no history beyond the day
before yesterday, an enormous restlessness intrudes. The fascist
idea of action for the sake of action and, surpassing this, of
action as the catalyst of truth, becomes attractive. This insinu-
ates itself into the American psyche, a Romantic replacement
for the values of rational contemplation and achievement.
Searching for stability we come to resemble rats in a maze
within a mélange of militant everything, scurrying to avoid the
shock while attaining the cheese. Anxiety reverberates and the
music of revolution becomes a cacophony that finally denies
recognition and sensibility. The prevailing ethos turns into desperation and, inescapably, an enervating despair.

This orchestration of political themes—however inadver-
tent—implicitly supports the customary relationships of
power, status, and privilege. Still, as much of humanity en-
deavors to emulate the American example of the liberal revolution, a more egalitarian revolution also proceeds. We need
to assimilate the pervading point that a nation moving toward
the capture of state authority by the monopolistic and oligopolistic grip of corporatist enterprise, which excels at what it
does best, the accumulation of venture capital—an actual subversion of the economics of a revolutionary liberalism which is
generically entrepreneurial—is also responding to a revolution beyond liberalism: a democratic revolution which, while
always a minor chord, is indisputably integral to the rhythms
of the American self.

In these contending revolutionary expectations the United
States manifests the concordance of opposites which com-

prises the whole. Within the contradiction, the red-scare ebbs
and flows, now approaching full tide once more as the accepted order of power continues to react against the memory
of the 1960s, seeking a version of the past which will gratify its
ardent longing to return. This finds expression in a quasi-
automatic fixation on "socialism," which will lose little intensity because of recent occurrences in Eastern Europe and what
was the Soviet Union, occurrences which have less to do with
"markets" than with the organized productivity of science and
technology.

With little doubt, the goal of protecting corporate profits,
thereby ensuring technocratic size and, accordingly, status
and power, has been historically pivotal to the values and attitudes of a political culture which is profoundly technological.
It is a goal that infuses the content of what now becomes a
military state in a fundamental economic sense: yielding an
obtuse penchant to reward the squandering of scientific and
technological talent, as well as of vast quantities of available
wealth, on war preparations[1] in an attempt to guarantee that
established power arrangements aren't distorted by the policy
consequences of a more egalitarian distribution of such
wealth. This has been accompanied, of course, by an impressive array of congressional and bureaucratic investigations,
and of commission after commission, blue-ribbon or otherwise, convened to fabricate an official statement of national
purpose.

But, in terms of ideology, what this panorama actually tells
us is that the sought-for balance of the American system is
grounded in an incessant desire to recover a free market
within a multinational corporatist world: a perverse mandate
against history[2] which defines all that is "progressive" as it simultaneously motivates all "reaction."

Only within the context of this world do Americans perceive
the feasibility of equilibrium: that informing conception of
group interaction reflecting the classical liberal conviction
that human fulfillment is best achieved through a business

"pluralism" as extolled by essential bourgeois agreements. Not surprisingly, the liberal inclination is often progressive in reference to the expansion of "human rights," and even "civil liberties," as long as "property rights" are respected and an unquestioned loyalty to "free enterprise" isn't disturbed.

However, the necessities of modern economics move in opposition to this comforting ambition, concentrating productive capacity into larger and larger units controlled by fewer and more transnational hands. What must evolve, for a people who admire both free markets and technology, is a cynical contortion of political vision and a looking inward that works to eradicate any progressive societal intention.

In an epoch when organized science becomes crucially fused with technological and economic expansion, the international flavor of revolution becomes more notable. Hence, to a greater extent than ever before, the struggles that centrally characterize the century must be addressed from a global perspective. Still, they often appear as magnified and more intensely focused in the United States. This is because the dream of "American exceptionalism" continues to be prevalent, not only in this country but—either as a positive or negative pronouncement—throughout much of the planet. Accordingly, while the movement of the 1960s wasn't contained by national boundaries, its American expression consistently attracts the greatest attention and comment and our translation of this movement comes to exemplify what is really the prevailing dialectic of contemporary Western history.

As the report to the Trilateral Commission regarding the United States described the events of the sixties, this was a time when those not previously articulate were suddenly clamoring to be heard, a decade when a multiplying array of groups were making claims on a constitutional structure that was calibrated to function well only for those few interests which presumably contributed to the "general welfare." Such a situation had to lead to overload and, not surprisingly, to a vast disappointment with government itself. What becomes clear is a portrait of a nation seething with voters possessing too much material affluence or, at least, the expectation of affluence, and who, as a consequence, have moved from "private" to "public" concerns while remaining inordinately ignorant of the historical purposes of a constitutional order.[3]

Here was a "democratic distemper" which, the report subtly suggested, could be alleviated by policies that decreased the living standards of most people, not by wage and salary reductions—which might provoke a troublesome response—but, as it turned out, through a scheme of inflationary pricing which employed the market power of the corporate "sector," along with the inventing and increasing of "fees" in the public "sector." This was an effort which a population saturated in an entrepreneurial ideology would interpret as the capricious workings of the true principles of economics.[4]

With the 1970s and the Nixon administration, this became the official, if unstated, position on how to ease the supposedly undue pressure on the political system. Concealed behind the amplifying electoral dynamics of the "social issues" of the time, it neatly avoided dealing with the elitist predilections of a country wherein the quest for privilege in the name of property rights is the uncompromising concern of the "successful." In this manner, liberal opportunity—and the permanent material scarcity upon which it is predicated—was advanced through policies which were economically depressive[5] and, concurrently, the immediate cause of a condition which now suffocates progressive thinking in the United States.

A decade later, this approach reached its apex during the "Reagan Revolution," an approach again made effective by the fact that there was no operative price-competitive market and that decision making by "private" companies dominated the expected patterns and internal details of "public" policy. If a sense of justified greed shaped the major contours of the Reagan years, and if more refined rationalizations applauded the greater availability of venture capital for domestic uses—which never happened but was their announced intent—the actual thrust of the 1980s was to further consolidate power. The nation thus turned away from the greater diversification of civic influence achieved in the 1960s which, while not democracy, is what the egalitarian impulse hidden within a technobureaucratic system necessitates.

Plainly, the advice of the Trilateral Commission was well conceived and well applied by a corporatist regime against the threat of countervailing power. It provides the economic basis of the present Thermidor. And, after all, worrying about and scurrying after money—whether we have a little of it or not—is reassuring to the American tradition. Despite the availability of affluence, this is now reinstated as the salient national posture. It certainly succeeds in keeping the vast majority of us fighting each other for monetary scraps and out of politics[6]—where we obviously don't belong.

Yet our refusal to acknowledge our endemic preference for a financial elitism leads to a persistent crisis, a crisis which in America reaches far back into the reflexes of the nation. It is implicit in a nervousness about political identity that is rampant in the reaction to the upheavals of the French Revolution, and in other guises during an earlier colonial experience. Similar attitudes, to be sure, are found in many places. But nowhere else is it woven into the fabric of the consciousness of a population in so contradictory a fashion. This becomes a critical preoccupation of the American outlook: a mind-set that even infiltrates assertions about "traditional values" that, to say the least, begin to appear a bit grandiose and, in their most extreme extensions, messianic as greed is increasingly exposed not as "productivity," but merely as greed. The need to discover the shadow partner in the troubled dance of elitism and equality patently impinges upon the American understanding of what revolution and counterrevolution are actually about.

He played a thousand tank towns. Then he made it big. But most people don't make it big. They play tank towns forever.

Nothing succeeds like success. We should all be famous for fifteen minutes, as Andy Warhol put it. Still, success, for us, is a fleeting joy. It can't sustain the needs of the psyche and leads to an ever reaching for more because this kind of success only serves status and emulation, and such attainment is not true to the person. Real joy is in producing. Along with civic effect, what Veblen called "the instinct of workmanship"[7] is the seedbed of all profound gratification: work that serves the need for inner value and self-worth, in the sense, as some of the ancient Greeks had it, of movement toward the fulfillment of the telos, of the more individuated and positive possibilities within people that compose the good life and makes human existence worthwhile.

Here is a condition which "'involves no ulterior motive for work other than the product being made and the processes of its creation'"; wherein those who labor are "at work and play in the same act" and who, accordingly, do "not try to escape from work into the sphere of leisure"; a condition in which "it is essential that the craftsman recognize the broader social meaning that his work possesses by grasping the moral and political implications of his work for the society in which he lives."[8] However, where the ideology of the market predominates, most people labor for the exchange value in the form of wages and salaries and, even within a corporatist reality, the purported capitalist strives for greater profits to be used as exchange value for status and the power that leads to privilege.

Indeed, the liberal mentality ensures that exchange value virtually becomes a surrogate for dignity and recognition. But these are human needs that finally require the power of freedom if they are to be realized at all. In its absence, people become alienated from nature, from others, and from themselves, while only labor which is not alienated, but free, can begin to rectify the distortions which typify the history of the species. Yet this isn't success as Americans understand it. We love to admire and to be admired. Nevertheless, actual success is only found in doing, and most of us do tank towns. And we can only look for the expression of ourselves, those elusive particles of gratification and affirmation, in the act of so doing.

Within this is discovered the economic foundation of any serious egalitarian argument.[9] Liberals seek social and political emulation, which they attach to the holding of wealth. But democrats seek the interior person through the realization of workmanship, in labor for use value, and in corresponding action in the polis which, unlike the most famous of the Greeks,[10] they think all are equally capable of attaining.

It follows that in a petit-bourgeois land democracy is never a popular position. Despite this, it creeps up on us as the income realities of equal opportunity become more blatant and the implications of the enormity of the available abundance are more generally apprehended.

Still, creeping up takes a while. To be young, and to be a product of the popular delusions of corporatist media and the educational system, is to be enamored of the mystification of property and of opportunity as the chance to get rich. But few get truly affluent, and hardly any get rich, and when they do they face a lack of public relevance and social rejection by people who inherit substantial amounts of money, along with that puzzling absence of gratification and an insistent boredom that even those of more respectable wealth share. Some try to justify their consequent frustration through the overt elitism of a right-wing politics which assures them that human aspirations are limited to what they have compiled, and that their having compiled it is sufficient evidence that they are superior to just about everyone else.[11] Here again, as always, an obstinate commitment to the past provides the rationale for a regressive inclination. It hardly matters. Tank towns or big time, liberal alienation from the self is integral to the American revolutionary theme.

So those who don't play tank towns, those who everyone agrees are at the top of the heap, never have enough. Lucre doesn't satisfy them while their avarice appears insatiable. The outcome is an adamant desire to get more as a glaring jingoism testifies to the strength of the political reaction they inferentially lead: an ambience avidly embraced by those who aren't successful in American terms, but who are ideologically sure that they, or their children, can be. This becomes manifest, within the present context, in a fear of the disturbing policy effects of the 1960s and, in a deeper sense, a petit-bourgeois nervousness about the very conception of political equality. Most significantly, however, it betrays a concern that the slumbering Jeffersonian predilection within the national memory may awaken once again: a tenacious reality that, so far, will not fade into historical oblivion, and which stirs at moments that are extremely inconvenient, not only to the present-day Whigs, but also to their compatriots, those Jacksonian practitioners of American "success."

The commercial elitism of the liberal revolution is softened by the certainty that the opportunity to accumulate wealth and status is open and equal. Throughout our history there have been periodic challenges to this assertion—sometimes on the grounds that the claim of equal entrepreneurial opportunity is a lie—more rarely by pointing out that the idea inherently determines that only material accumulation is worth attaining, and that this alone violates the democratic conception of opportunity as actualization through an equality of freedom as a reflection of an equality of civic power. Both critiques deeply informed the presiding episodes and contentions of the sixties: episodes and contentions which were shaped by the pressures of conflict between liberalism and democracy—a focus on emancipation in contrast to a quest for the power necessary to freedom. Thus does the slogan of "democracy" now and then rebound against those who use it as a technique of class and elite rule, occasions which interfere with that ability to manage events which emanates from an assumable ideological cohesion.

In this manner liberty is counterposed to equality, as though inequality exacts no price from liberty. The contradiction herein expressed is as old as America. It spans generational differences, and we must understand this if we are to comprehend ourselves. Yet, for a people nourished on "constitutional-democracy," such comprehension is really beyond the bearing of it. It follows that those who vocalize the intellectual content of the received political wisdom reject any serious attempt to engage in a theoretical effort which might allow a more scientific appreciation of the process of human and societal development, which people desire, and which ultimately represents a universal aspiration that moves history. In the interim, we who play endless tank towns can search for a larger civic purpose, and a pride in what the political order is supposed to be, only within those expected affirmations that are available upon demand.

Anyway, how do you make a revolution when everybody has their own racket going—and why bother?

A nation of sellers is reflexively a nation of buyers, and that which radiates from this preeminent business relationship—replete with a rich complexity of activity and the rampant conceptual simplicity of "economic man"—are the real values so acclaimed by those whose professional charge it is to celebrate the genius of the system. These suffuse a population engrossed in the pursuit of personal material gain and in a willingness to labor for enough to invest and to exist off the labor of others: not truly for the enjoyment of what money might do, but for the opportunity to make more. Such is the fruition of our "revolution," one which magnifies the techniques of merchandising into those congealing agreements woven into the fabric of the American "community" and the stuff of the American dream.

The land of opportunity; the great leveling promise at the center of our experience; justifying wealth distributions as "earned" and, accordingly, proper—the composition of revolution as Americans apprehend and typically applaud it in myriad "opinion" polls, elections, referenda, and other ballot returns. Still, this connection between opportunity and revolution is not unique. Some idea of human opportunity is always the energizing inspiration behind the restless motion of revolution and reaction.

What we failed to appreciate in the 1960s is that traditional agreements about the source of economic value, and of its proper distribution,[12] invariably control the content and arrangements of power and authority. But this only reveals an anterior conception of opportunity that, in turn, emerges from the possibilities of material production as perceived by a critical mass of those involved. And, when a particular meaning of opportunity comes to be dominant among a population it fosters a preeminent consciousness which is made tangible through its stipulations about what kind of behavior is worthy of recognition and, most often, of the awarding of dignity. This finds expression in social esteem, an empirically discernible phenomenon which has the effect of creating and distributing power and authority. Hence the road to power is determined by a permeating notion of opportunity rooted in a common understanding of technological feasibilities, a construction which indirectly generates power by delegating psychological authority, as well as those formal commands on loyalty known as political authority, to those who are most successful in its terms.

America, it is contended, has never made up its mind whether its "revolution" was about liberty or money.[13] This decision has, however, been made, at least so far, because liberty is ideologically transformed into monetary achievement, and private wealth acquisition long suppresses any identifiable alternative in regard to the national commitment. Nevertheless, a steadily advancing affluence, which can't be kept completely secret and, therefore, to some degree, must be made more widely available, works, in the aggregate, to weaken the deference, status, and resulting power and privilege to which personal financial aggrandizement is historically entitled. The impact of diminishing marginal utility becomes more severe as people begin to discover that additional lucre doesn't necessarily enhance liberty. Most directly, they more often must choose between a further gain in income and any semblance of the power of freedom that can only be actualized through workmanship and public effect.

The dream of liberal revolution is of the financial attainment released by an entrepreneurial order that will eventuate in a republic and an environment conducive to citizenship. If this was ever true, it is no longer. Tremendous concentrations of capital flow from a centralized control of wealth production, turning citizens into consumers and consumers into subjects and electorates into audiences, thereby encouraging the buying of elections with "public" illusions that are manufactured and sold. It is not enough to drop out and escape to a rural commune in Colorado, or to demonstrate that one is a devotee of Adam Smith by living on the beach and making sandals and selling them to tourists while buying leather from what is in all probability a subsidiary of Armour or Swift. What the 1960s exposed is a national reality that can't continue to be cavalierly avoided through the simple announcement that history is on our side[14] and by an insistent invocation of the language of equal opportunity as a "right." As "publics" and "factions" are translated into "masses," and elections into plebiscites, it becomes apparent that individual liberty and, more profoundly, freedom, can only derive from a pluralism predicated, not upon a capitalist market that is nowhere to be found, but upon a comprehension of the scientific and technological dynamics and nuances of existing power—and of the values, attitudes, and perceptions which infuse the sovereign ideology of opportunity and bring about these dynamics and nuances.

This is the historical meaning of the 1960s. Because of it there has been a dedicated establishment effort to convince the American people that nothing that matters happened during that decade. And, from the perspective of the current Thermidor, it does appear that the movement of that time was of little real consequence. It certainly didn't change the values and attitudes that exemplify the American order, and which find their most vital expression in an unrequited affection for "equal opportunity."

Clearly, the resilience of a transnational corporatist system, and the entreprenurial consciousness behind which it operates, and which lends it overwhelming psychological authority, was much tougher and more intractable than we thought. If the political appeal of capitalism was the liberty to be your own boss, its enduring economic appeal wasn't markets, but the technological sophistication of productive technique which price competition and the law of supply and demand would bring to the globe. Although Hamilton had ascertained quite early that wealth production is far more enhanced by a concentration of economic power than by an entrepreneurial diversity—a view which is plain in his policy of "promotionalism" for major commercial firms—this was understood by few in America until the last quarter of the nineteenth century. By then it was becoming apparent to some that technological advance was being fettered by capitalism and that a deliberate coordination of large capital with government was the price of rapid, or even further, material achievement.

Unnoticed by a nation ideologically enamored with the market revolution of liberalism, it is precisely the end of free enterprise and the transition to the interlock of corporate planning with state and national policies which propels the accelerated production of goods and services in the United States during the twentieth century. The era of capitalism—to the degree it ever really existed—was actually a staging ground for the technical leaps in economic yield that epitomize postindustrial systems. Yet the truth is that today even the Left rarely perceives any of this to be a result of the dominance of a free market that realized its promised productivity by transforming itself into something else: a global and technocratic mercantilism of astounding wealth that can well afford to mitigate the more extreme instances of the material exploitation of labor power historically associated with entrepreneurial activity.

But not only were we dense about the capacity of the technocracy to neutralize criticism and resistance. Of far greater importance, we didn't comprehend why it had become so powerful in the first place. The pivotal contradiction of capitalism, as Marx pointed out, is its very success in rendering the techniques of production more efficient,[15] a feat that now carries with it the imperatives of enormous investment and long-range planning: imperatives that are compatible only with large organizations and bureaucratic structures that can't be contained within free markets. What ramifies is an impressive technological progress which requires less and less labor engaged in a transnational enterprise which is characteristically governed by the paramount position of fewer and fewer companies roaming the world in quest of resources and cheaper costs for that labor still relevant to production. Where the outcome isn't a condition of outright monopoly, it is one of oligopoly,[16] or "imperfect competition": a system of power as well as economics that dictates what liberal opportunity means in contemporary America.

As long as people have to derive an income within these constrictions there can be little freedom in the land of the free. Thus the market becomes an arcane social myth which America is eager to transport to the greater world as a cloak for corporatist supremacy while actual entrepreneurial opportunity diminishes. With an accelerating consistency, the financial opportunity which still exists represents a chance to serve those technobureaucratic values which find concrete expression in the priorities of public policy in the United States.

Despite our historical affinity for a market "individualism," it is increasingly evident that we dwell within a domain wherein capitalist activity is viable only on the fringes of the order—and typically, for a magnifying array of industries, only for a while—a domain wherein most people possess no noticeable ability to affect what is understood to be the public realm. Such is an America, as Norman Thomas suggested some years ago, in which the only real capitalists are small boys playing marbles for keeps. Yet, all of this notwithstanding, the ultimate concern of the radicalism of the 1960s devolved into an attempt to introduce an expansion of equal opportunity into the moral, economic, intellectual, and political "markets."[17]

Without a doubt, this was a progressive inclination. But what we missed were the intrinsic connections between our own ideology and our conception of revolution: never realizing that swelling the ranks of participants in a corporatist America changed nothing about the components and configurations of power, while literally amplifying the insidious reach of a consciousness that permits opportunity to be understood only in technobureaucratic terms. Corporate control, not by owners, but by managers[18] and, now, technostructures,[19] was accordingly bolstered through a translation of entrepreneurial opportunity into the opportunity to perform corporate labor: a translation made complete by the conflating of entertainment and celebrity with citizenship. Not to grasp this was a substantial failure of analysis. It was to try to make a revolution without a theory complex enough to deal with the power realities we were facing—and this can never be.

Hence, we became reactive to events instead of to historical consistencies. Finally, in frustration, we turned inward and away from being political in any systemic manner. That which couldn't be changed without an adequate theoretical grasp of the magnitude of what we were confronting led us to personal concerns and even excesses, violent or otherwise—the present media portrayal of a selfish and immature decade—as the sixties and early seventies ended and the eightiesloomed to retrieve the solace of a financially defined sense of "worth."

At our best we became preoccupied with local "communities," ignoring the triumphant arrival of "the twentieth-century capitalist revolution"—a "revolution" that gives us a multinational corporatism within which all smaller communities are effectively subsumed. Not only did we fail to observe that giant "private" firms had become social institutions[20] or, more explicitly, "private governments."[21] We were also oblivious to the corresponding impact of our own socialization to the technocratic values of an "entrepreneurial" America. And we didn't know what to do with our better hunches which hazily suggested that somewhere within the configurations of corporatist power lingered the possibilities of a new and more human conception of opportunity: that this might be a derivation of the productive stipulations of material abundance.

These are failures that persist. The Left continues to misinterpret the abiding values and attitudes that shape the monetary perceptions and behavior which comprise the core of American stability. Too often, it searches for bad guys and good guys instead of for the logic of economic agreements which impels people to behave in ways they otherwise wouldn't: a logic of concentration which doesn't maintain a balance among entrepreneurs freely entering and leaving markets, but which instead devours entrepreneurs and relentlessly shrinks their numbers relative to the entire "market." And, in a reverse twist, a twist which persuasively expresses its present confusion, the Left is hardly even alert to what Arendt so correctly pointed out, that the attempt to apply capitalist ideas in any part of the earth wherein natural resources aren't exceptionally abundant has invariably led to economic devastation.[22] The scenario is what it must be—a myopic distortion of a force that now imposes disturbing permutations upon the supposed market parameters of the national political scene.

Such are the realities of "the commercial republic" which

lurk beneath those slogans that promote "equal opportunity" and a pervasive American belief in the conclusive equation of "capitalism and freedom."[23]

8. Democracy, Thermidor, and the Forces of History

The free-speech movement. Participatory democracy. Black Power. The flower children and Yippies and pot heads and the urgent claims of the counterculture. Love that became rage and finally mere rivulets of an apparent irrelevance, fueling a national mood of despair and dislocation. The closing of the "credibility gap" followed by the regression of the 1980s, a decade when Americans literally believed that material wealth was produced by the aggrandized acquisitiveness of the few and not by the labor of scientific discovery and a consequent technological innovation. And now the broken promises of the "market" arrive, predictably bringing with them the cynicism which accompanies a seemingly irreducible debt, and "restructuring" and "downsizing"—along with a greater concentration of a corporatist mercantilism on a transnational stage.

So the devotees of established power breathe a sigh of relief at the immobility of progressive predilections: at the fact that the 1960s have purportedly ended. But they are nervous about it. And, they should be as the anger and distrust on the fringes of the system creep inexorably toward the center, and as the vector of transformation finds conversion in new alliances that are merely the most immediate outward manifestations of those pervading contradictions which reflect the restlessness of the species.

Revolution invariably proceeds in convulsive surges and apparent retreats that become coherent only when perceived as the pathways of a larger and often invisible movement that imposes grudging change upon the greater eventualities of human existence. These are the forces of history, an articulation—sometimes stated but far more frequently implied—of the needs and desires of populations which are deemed to carry the weight of historical significance. And it was in this arena that we missed the causes of the situation we were confronting: as well as of the kind of resistance always associated with important social transition. We preferred instead to yearn for an idealized version of the past—itself a powerful political reality. In this, we revealed a reflexive desire for the familiar and perhaps, in a deeper dialectical sense, and regardless of the confusion and pain that usually attends it, for the exuberance of our own youth—always a quiet feature of revolution[1] within the opaque story of human development on both a personal and societal scale.

Yet, whatever our motivations, the issue of historical forces can't be avoided. It is what those who are conditioned to the parochial references of a specific generation must address in terms that are adequate to the substance and operative energies of the world they inhabit. Each thrust forward of the "cycle" of revolutionary change is paramount to those who live in that time. But the greater material motion of which it is a part is easily lost to perception—especially when the anticipated reaction occurs.

Aware of it only dimly, if at all, those who struggled for a more democratic America in the 1960s were driven by ideas propagated by the left wing of the eighteenth-century European Enlightenment. Here was the conviction that the shackles of wealth deprivation and regressive political habits could be broken and that more egalitarian possibilities could finally begin to be released through the discovery and application of the reason of natural law. Still, those who adhered to this contention in the sixties misunderstood too much. The democratic argument was historically agrarian in its physiocratic base, predicated upon the economics and simple technology of small farming. Any feasible application to industrial and postindustrial conditions was never seriously considered in America because this could incite a Marxian inclination—

which is patently off limits in a nation so engulfed by a Lockian consciousness that it can tolerate no competing analysis of the content of the human disposition.

In this manner, the anathema of "Marxism" has long prevented even American "radicals" from truly entertaining the theory that revolution may not be endless cyclical repetition, or a linear vector in a progressive direction, but a gradually increasing awareness that we aren't what we are capable of being as this becomes clarified within the spiraling motion of a dialectical history. Such, indeed, is an alien thought. Yet people like the very American Thorstein Veblen have also never been acceptable to the monolithic certainties of American liberalism. Plainly not permitted as well is a view of revolution that emerges from the conception of contradiction which infuses ideas of evolution:[2] a view which postulates that all species, including human beings, are in the process not merely of actualizing a nature which was always within, but are part of a transmutation whereby sufficient development causes them to cease being what they are and to turn into something they never were. In short, those who theorized for the movement of the sixties typically avoided the more complicated extensions of the Enlightenment that resonate from the second half of the nineteenth century: extensions which infer that the problem of historical forces must be recognized as fundamental to the substantive concerns of all politics.

Trying to glimpse where we are from within the gloom of the present Thermidor, we await the next "revolutionary" explosion. And, unaware of the essential fact that the concordance of opposites has become central to a scientific approach to reality; caught in accounts of history as cycles or straight and elevating lines; we remain persuaded that the present response to the 1960s means that we've lost all we thought had been achieved. Careful attention to the dominant debates of the current political scene should disabuse us of this. However, we don't really listen, and a debilitating pessimism becomes de rigueur among those committed to a progressive agenda. They are increasingly impressed by the allegedly innate deficiencies which control the political capacities of most people, to the point where the liberal order is proclaimed to be "the end of history,"[3] the indisputable summit of political achievement: an outlook that is now soberly agreed to by many who fought the battles of the sixties.

Such is the restrictive insularity of the American consciousness, wherein all positions on the political spectrum are subsumed into a liberal formulation of history: a formulation which has never resolved its commitment to a linear notion of progress with its more than equal attraction to the assurance that human history unavoidably returns to a functional equivalency of what came before. Despite the required liberal references to "progress" as the discovery of rights, this easily becomes the pronouncement that the only tangible progress is an augmented opportunity to accumulate private wealth by contributing to the material output of technology, while the interior qualities of the personality, beset by a tension between reason and passion, maintain a static consistency. Every aspect of the human psyche, other than the desire for money, is thus fixed by a relative balance regulated by this tension: a balance which allegedly varies little within each individual—although these differences apparently become vital when attempting to identify who the members of the economic and, thereby, the political meritocracy really may be.

It follows that the generic predilections of the species guarantee that progress is an illusion. What appears to be advance in regard to the inner person must be succeeded by a time which signifies the initial step toward a deterministic restoration of the status quo ante: a judgment that freezes the liberal proposal of opportunity as market position into the only kind of opportunity compatible with human nature.[4] Revolution becomes an adamant return to a balanced order, a "fact" which even the Left in a Lockian America now implicitly accepts as "realistic"—and, quite frequently, preferable.

Such is the perspective of the Thermidor, a perspective which is afforded intellectual currency by writers like Crane Brinton,[5] who uses it to describe the vicissitudes of the British, American, French, and Soviet revolutions. It asserts a claim that attains the flavor of inevitability which informs most recent attempts to explore the densities of revolution—inferring, when it doesn't overtly insist, that the Thermidor announces the beginning of the recovery of previously prevailing values and attitudes, along with the composition and delegations of power and authority which constitute their tangible political result. Hence revolutions are rare occurrences of a definable duration: unique events that represent temporary abnormalities within the general panorama of species existence. "Thermidor comes as naturally to societies in revolution as an ebbing tide, as calm after a storm, as convalescence after fever, as the snapping-back of a stretched elastic band." It is an inherent constituent of the episodic upheavals that a nation sometimes endures: running their course through the cyclical formations of fanaticism, Thermidor, and "Restoration," leaving the social organism essentially unchanged although, perhaps, a bit "strengthened by the experience."[6]

Since Brinton is describing much while theorizing little, the question of explanatory power isn't especially relevant here. Nevertheless, the very meaning of the Thermidor, which must depict the elitist nature of rule as never changing—at least for long—can be critically misleading. It is suggestive that Brinton admits to notable difficulties when applying the conception of the Thermidor, as well as of the succeeding Restoration, to the American example, perhaps because the ex-colonies in North America conclusively avoided a revolution after 1776. But of far greater importance is Brinton's little-discussed last chapter, in which he conjectures that the seemingly endless stages of a revolving process may be nothing more than large events within a far-greater and continuing revolution. Those who adhere to his viewpoint consistently ignore this because they ignore Brinton's speculation that, despite the cyclical patterns of revolutions, a certain degree of unexplained and lasting change does occur. This he roughly identifies as a transition from preindustrial to industrial societies,[7] an identification which may reveal that when dealing with the phenomenon of revolution it is difficult to avoid Marx, no matter how hard one tries. And Brinton certainly does try.

It is, of course, conceivable that the "moderation" of the Thermidor and the regressive qualities of the Restoration, while real, aren't actually confirmations of a return to an earlier condition: that, indeed, the retrieval of a prior time in terms of opportunity and power isn't a serious probability. To this proportion, what looms as the equivalence of retreat is most likely to be a sorting out of the effects of traumatically progressive episodes.[8] And, accordingly, the "neoconservative" domination of American politics since the 1960s might well be an indication of the residue which always trails in the wake of revolutionary efforts that attain a discernible level of success.

The working out of the movements for civil rights, opposition to imperialistic military adventures, environmentalism, and the expansion of equality for women is likely to be messy, while the champions of counterrevolution can be expected to be loud and well financed—and heavily armed with an array of conventional truths which are alluringly palatable and readily digested. During such times, the voices of social wisdom avidly deny possibility, even as they concurrently applaud the general human weaknesses that demand pessimism, regression, and the loss of larger historical ambition. This appears, at least for a while, to be the only "reasonable" position. To appreciate the profound restrictions on the characteristic human capacity for rational thought and action becomes political "sophistication"—a designation reminiscent of the "realism" of the 1950s, the years of Thermidor following the unsettling disruptions of the 1930s and early 1940s and the great egalitarian thrust of countervailing power during the New Deal era. It is this attitude which now infuses the authoritative responses to the 1960s, voiced as a troubled assurance that the golden age of tradition must be reached for and recovered.

"As I would not be a slave, so I would not be a master. This expresses my idea of democracy. Whatever differs from this, to the extent of the difference, is no democracy."

Within these mediations of Lincoln resides a doctrine which is more indispensable and difficult than it might at first appear. Few want to be slaves. So much for the easy part. But despite, as Hegel indicated, the interconnection between the two,[9] the desire to be a master, to have power over instead of power to,[10] is an enduring feature of human history. To try to break with this ingrained behavior is to begin to come to grips with the democratic meaning of equality; that each is no worse than any other, and also no better; that we are all noble and we all stink the same; that we can't look up to others and we can't look down in any manner that speaks to being qualified to rule.[11] If we possess a diversity of useful talents each, to the extent it is realized, is equally necessary to the ability of the species to prosper, since variation is the condition of its further evolution and, therein, the individuation of its membership and its own continued survival. This is as crucial to the democratic understanding of revolution as it is nearly impossible for a liberal people to accept as an accurate portrayal of the human situation. In contrast to our much-proclaimed affection for "democracy," we find it rather simple, and ultimately more comfortable, to attach ourselves to one or more of the many nuances on the traditional theme of political elitism: a theme that effectively distorts the experience of revolution—so far.

Thus, we come to consider "progress" and "reform" as steps back to what preceded because it is only this that the American insistence on a liberal balance will allow. To think otherwise is to indulge in delusion. It is to risk evoking the enervating "Muse" of futility and despair. A return to entrepreneurial pursuits is that which sensibly remains to any who comprehend the circumscribed nature of a being who can't tolerate "revolution" on any other terms.

And all the while the price of this reactionary fantasy gets higher as the momentum of a vaguely discerned force moves a liberal nation further away from what, in fact, it once was.

9. "Equal Opportunity" and the Nineteen-Sixties

What Tocqueville saw so clearly and, in the final analysis, feared, was democracy as a historical force—that which he wanted to "educate" into a respect for "reason" and, by virtue of this, for government by the competing rational elites of the liberal formulation. Nowhere else has such "education" been as overwhelmingly successful as in a Lockian America—at least as long as entrepreneurial opportunity appears feasible. But this is to be expected among a petit-bourgeois people who think they are bourgeois: an interlude, perhaps, in the emanation of a more egalitarian consciousness which, in its essential development, as Tocqueville realized, can't really be stopped.

It is instructive, as Jimmy Breslin so cogently put it, that those who wield power amidst the triumphant return of the commercial republic to the United States are "scared shitless of the movement." They have excellent reason to be. Infusing the chaos and action of the 1960s, and exceeding the release of an outrage too long repressed, the great revelation of that time was that those who never mattered might actually matter after all, that the secret was that there was no secret:[1] a revelation which is always the guiding ethos and informing discovery propelling that egalitarian expansion of power and authority which epitomizes revolution. The Kafkaesque Castle of a corporatist America was presumably immune to any influence but its own. Nonetheless, although not destroyed, the Castle was dangerously assaulted. Its ramparts were breached; its vulnerabilities exposed; its inhabitants severely shaken. Plainly, they are acutely alert to further disturbances; far slicker and less overt and heavy-handed in the way they behave, now breaking with the normal vocabulary of capitalist rhetoric by talking about investment opportunities not in terms of profitability, but in the language of employment; more willing to replace their usual arrogance with the appearance of accommodating to pressures they still don't quite comprehend.

These pressures are felt because out of the furor of the sixties evolved an early, if murky, conception of systemic opportunity that is more essentially human than entrepreneurial acquisition: a conception that suddenly appears attractive to more and more people. Regardless of periodic reversals, throughout this century, as material abundance indisputably advances, the goal of civic effect intrudes upon the goal of money and a need for the power requisite to freedom becomes an increasingly audible demand. This, not rights, is what "relevance" really means, and its attempted denial can lead to cynicism only when such a demand is already real.

The imposition of military force is an overt and often brutal event. But force is coercion, not power, because power is influence rooted in common perceptions and, finally, consent, while coercion indicates an absence of power precisely because it represents an absence of ideological approval by a critical mass of those involved.[2] Such is an oblique sociological reality that manifests a consensus about values, and about those pervasive attitudes that are actually clues to values of which we are not aware.

Any constellation of values and attitudes is predicated upon a bundle of hunches about human proclivities which ultimately congeal into a notion of opportunity. And power, as well as legal power, or political authority, must reflect the prevailing ideology about opportunity because we confer "success" according to the particular agreements which this ideology articulates. In this manner we identify those worthy of dignity and of being admired and emulated and, by the act of doing so, we create power and authority. Certainly, the need for power—for effect in reference to both the self and the greater world—is a pivotal component of human existence. Yet the source of its specific expression is always revealed through accepted formulations about the nature of opportunity.

Hence the ingredients and parameters of opportunity become a reliable indicator of those values and attitudes that delineate the order and command consent. And, since it is opportunity which dictates the substance and arrangements of the power and authority that constitute the political system, we strive for position and privilege only within the conformities thus established.

Of course, force is often employed to destroy novel ideas of opportunity, or to weaken the power they may yield. Nonetheless, as Rousseau infers, regimes that resist a new and tenacious portrayal of success on the basis of force are of brief tenure unless, as John Stuart Mill further surmises, the endurance of such regimes is bolstered by military intervention from outside. But power can never impede opportunity because it is the general perception of the content of opportunity which literally controls the operative limits and actual qualities of power itself.

We are all acculturated to a particular version of opportunity, as we are born into the fact that the promise of opportunity and the force of revolution are inseparable. To want in on the deal is reform or, in its most extreme instances, rebellion. To want more than the deal is the beginning of revolution. It is evident that revolutionary movements necessitate a seizure of, and a transformation in, the character and organization of power and authority. But this is a process which can only follow the emergence of a fuller and more egalitarian understanding of "human nature," an emergence which induces an amplifying range of discontent with the traditional version of opportunity. At these times, the chances for "success" appear to greater magnitudes of people to be illusory—and the connection of opportunity to revolution intrudes as visible and fundamental: a disclosure which historically contains the seeds of a more inclusively human consciousness.

Because those who advocated revolutionary change in the 1960s typically failed to recognize that some definition of opportunity is always the binding adhesive of the political order, as well as the basis of revolution against it, they strived for an outcome that couldn't be attained. The unquestioned commitment of the nation to opportunity as financial gain rendered anything else implausible and unrealistic. However, most who composed the movement of the sixties had difficulty identifying this generically American perspective within their own attitudes, encouraging a lack of historical vision which finally contorted their efforts—not allowing them to comprehend revolution in a deeper and empirically more realistic sense. Hence, the call for "relevance" which, at first, made a claim on power, rapidly diminished into an argument for a more equitable distribution of bourgeois "rights," especially as these were anchored in presiding liberal commitments about the relationship of private rights to productive property. The battles of the sixties increasingly revolved around "social policies" fought out in the parlance of the rational elitism of the Constitution and capitalism and, while laudable at the time, the functional ability of the movement to confront the economic principles of the order never surpassed this to any significant degree. This was because, in the end, the radicalism of the decade missed the critical stipulations of democratic opportunity in reference to both labor and citizenship.

These are stipulations which transcend concerns about status and deference, recognition and esteem, position and privilege, because they inherently address the more profound motivations of human beings: the abiding need to matter in the world; to arrive at the activation of freedom as public power; ambitions that the capitalist constrictions of a liberal ideology can never permit to be truly realized because they mandate not a commercial "individualism," but the economic and technological preconditions of an egalitarian politics. It is this contrast between liberalism and democracy which starkly illuminates the fact that the Jeffersonian contention is much more a theory of power than a doctrine of rights, that without the power and authority of freedom that allows their exercise rights have no meaning, especially when they are used as the ideological justification for rule as designated by personal wealth accumulation. This is the case, moreover, even when delegations of authority allegedly reflect a proportionate contribution to material production which results from the proper management of those techniques of fabrication directly causal to such production. What ramifies is a tension between revolution as the opportunity for a monetary elitism and revolution as opportunity within an egalitarian distribution of the power actualized by action through unalienated labor and within the available space of politics.

Still, if we didn't know enough about the democratic principle of opportunity and, therefore, about its importance to any attempt to bring about revolutionary change in the dominant consciousness of a postindustrial population, we did hazily suspect that the issue of power couldn't be separated from that of liberty. "Power to the people," we thereby proclaimed, never noticing, however, that "the people" already possessed the foundations of power, and that their commitment to capitalist opportunity was what effectively ensured its apparently intractable history.

In any event, all we truly intended was a "restoration" of a liberal balance to the American order. Accordingly, the terms of our critique were grounded in a traditional liberal adherence to natural rights: the normative core of which was eloquently articulated by Warren and Brandeis as "the right to be let alone,"[3] the pervading assertion that liberty is escape from the power of others and, in a palpable sense, from the conditioned reactions and reflexive commands of the self. Presumably made possible by the natural workings of the entrepreneurial market here, in its most attractive and elevated exposition, was a return to the preeminent assumptions of the capitalist proposition: the possessive individualism of a Hobbesian and Lockian world view.

Yet exceeding economic liberty is the far-more human and

perplexing phenomenon of freedom, a dimension within which our perceptual difficulties became obvious because we were simply too liberal to apprehend the fundamental distinction between freedom and liberty. Freedom isn't an attempt to escape. It is, instead, the ability to affirm and, conclusively, to do so in a larger and more public arena. Such is the classical meaning of citizenship, and its extended application is the most likely road to the integrity of the polis—to which the democratic position adds the insistence that citizenship can't exist for any unless it works equally for all. Thus, while liberty is a release from power, freedom is explicitly power that becomes expressive of the fuller development of the self and others—of the positive predilections within people to act productively in the world[4] as these are enhanced through greater psychological integration and a view of opportunity that inspires a further equality in the very meaning and structure of power and authority. This, of course, is a development which is fully dependent upon a prior transformation in those systemically nurtured values and attitudes which generate the paramount notion of opportunity and suffuse it with the energy of historical effect.

Any theory of revolution has to be concerned with why this happens because, at bottom, this is the catalyst of revolution. And the values and attitudes of human beings empirically derive from those shared formulations which emanate from the way people discern what is universal, as well as from the way they think things ought to be. More distinctly than any discrete set of economic arrangements, these historically speak to the material conditions of existence: conditions which now introduce the issue of the corporate, bureaucratic, and implicitly authoritarian organization of production required by technological advance, as well as that of its incipient contradiction, the pluralistic and egalitarian organization and the open-ended values and imagination of the scientific enterprise as these are mediated through the universities and their associated institutions. This imposes a situation wherein technology concentrates power while science diversifies it, a constellation which is most graphically true in postindustrial nations wherein the contradiction is most extreme. And it is precisely within the opaque complexity of doctrines, theories, and behavior that these nations represent that we must look for that extant and emerging force that comprises the salient elements of modern revolution.

What this reveals is a history of dialectical tension that attends the ideological melding of science and technology, a tension which vitally characterizes the enormous transnational power that now engulfs the United States, and which translates entrepreneurial opportunity into the bureaucratic opportunities of corporatist interest. And it is exactly within the ideology of opportunity that the "aesthetic vision"[5]—which motivates scientific theory and empirical discovery—most patently clashes with the smoothly running routines and structured imperatives of technical invention and application. Such is a clash which contains reverberating implications for the entirety of American politics.

If, in the contemporary era, the doing of technology is an act of maintaining liberal supremacy, the doing of science becomes an essential act of democratic immersion into the world of power and the motion of freedom.[6] These increasingly represent a material contradiction which moves the major tendencies of our age in a more monolithic and a more egalitarian direction at the same time. Nevertheless, stubbornly mistaking technology for "capitalism," and twisting the snobbery and haughty demeanor of certain scientists into an elitist[7] claim to govern, those who wanted to bring revolutionary change to America in the 1960s failed to identify the subversive disposition within the prevailing force—the historical, transnational, and pluralizing disposition of a procedure of empirical verification open to all who want to participate.[8]

Herein lurks the primary contradiction within those matters of ideology, opportunity, and power that currently subsume the American system: realities with which the movement of the sixties couldn't contend. Those who took part were ultimately too American, too liberal, too Aristotelian and Newtonian, to even begin to suspect that a progressive force can exist only within the sovereign force, and our inability—and even refusal—to comprehend this assured that the actual basis of countervailing power would continue to effectively elude perception.[9]

Dispersed and, indeed, hoodwinked by a preoccupation with an equal "right" to pursue "private" wealth, we missed the central point that, to get past the continual panorama of insurrections, reforms, riots, putsches, civil wars, coups d'etat, acts of terror, and rebellions—to get to revolution—the constituents and configurations of opportunity and power, and of the values, attitudes, and perceptions which they echo, and which make them acceptable in specific places and times, must be the principal focus of political analysis. Power, like authority, is never taken; it is always given—by others or the self—in whatever combination. Values and attitudes revolving around opportunity produce power because they saturate and shape it, and the evolution of a resulting consciousness becomes the permeating truth of revolution. These are the ideological antecedents of the 1960s, as well as of the counterrevolution of the 1980s; that desire to return to a more "settled" time when it was "rationally" understood that the only legitimate progress was a greater opportunity to maximize personal wealth; a resounding reassertion of habit which found welcome support in a perverse rejection of the national turmoil of two decades before.

However—as is already becoming apparent—the 1980s were a diversion from the deeper consistencies of history. Human needs more various than monetary aggrandizement seek fuller expression once financial security can be plausibly and generally assumed. We search for ourselves and the universe and, through this effort, for our place within it. As a consequence, the creative power associated with self-generating and activating stimuli inexorably replaces the passive stimuli of an avaricious material consumption, disclosing a longing to affect the world in a manner that enhances and extends the story of the species. This involves a transition in the meanings of opportunity and exploitation, which become less preoccupied with debates about the stealing of labor time and more concerned with any use of people for purposes that are not actually their own.[10]

Thus expressed is the persistent direction of our experience: an exploration for the power of freedom that fades and seems to disappear only to be suddenly heard from again as the dialectical pattern of species development announces that the time for action in the polis by augmented numbers of people has once more arrived. So we are presently subsumed by monetary concerns, and the music of equality and fulfillment in labor and the political, which must accompany the movement toward individuation, is muted, for a while, and we revert to the opportunity of being financial animals: and the devotees of a market reaction can be smug about the "economic" essence of our nature. For a while.

10. The Subtle Persistence of the Nineteen-Sixties

It is probably appropriate to note the conjectures of Erich Fromm about the presumed conflict between pessimism and optimism. These are, he contends, intrinsically identical postures: abstractions detached from the contradictions of human needs and behavior, and from those actualizing aspirations which critically involve an engagement in the world.[1] For the pessimist, nothing can be done; for the optimist, nothing has to be done. Yet, as the 1960s revealed, what we do does matter. There are moments in history when a sensitivity to the deeper motivations of populations becomes vocalized in a systemic manner; moments that appear to be spasmodic and unconnected events; but which are really the more convulsive and dramatic instances of those spiraling themes of dialectical emergence which compose the quietly intrusive rythyms of revolutionary motion.

As it is difficult to observe coherently from the midst of the occurrence, it remains difficult to evaluate the political residue of the 1960s, even with the passage of years. Surely, as is well-known, historians prefer the hindsight of at least two or three centuries. Nevertheless, some temporal distance from what took place does promote a more refined identification of cause and effect, helping us to distill what might be significant from the ongoing turbulence of events.

It is already plain that the 1960s inspired what has become a seemingly unremitting crisis of authority, legitimacy, and purpose in a technobureaucratic system which the smart money assured us could never be meaningfully influenced. The legacy of the sixties—before we turned away from the polis and into our liberal selves—was to make "relevance," and its inferences for political authority, an enduring public issue for the first time in American history: a phenomenon comparable to the European revolutions of 1848 when those who sold their labor finally attained the level of a class identity.

Most specifically, the movement of the 1960s had historical importance because it exposed a configuration of power that couldn't be exposed: a stripping away of the ideological veils that cloak power, which is what serious political inquiry must always be about.[2] In this, the decade articulated an angle of approach that was quintessentially revolutionary. It dispersed a bit of the mist, partially uncovering a concentrated locus of de facto authority which was disguised by a constellation of regions and styles that generated no substantive policy differences, bringing to wider awareness the presiding interests, as well as the values and attitudes, that were served in the name of the "general welfare." Thus it was abruptly transparent that equal opportunity had become technocratic opportunity for the few born to—or absorbed into—at least the borders of privilege and station: that, somehow, the free market had become a corporate feudalism or, maybe more accurately, a corporate dynasty, which was typified not only by its own inordinate power, but by the ceaseless and bloated assurances that its ability to govern was best for us all.

As a result, America is now more frequently seen as a monolithic order that parades as a system of pluralism: a country wherein most people are left out of the power equation and, accordingly, devoid of citizenship in any operative sense. The anger and cynicism which this creates—although often misdirected—represents the egalitarian particle within the American consciousness counterposing itself to the imagined antipolitics[3] of an economic and transnational liberalism. What becomes evident is the informing Jeffersonian conviction that indispensable to democracy is a political independence that can't be achieved when masses of people are materially beholden to the financial and, now, the technocratic manipulations of the few.

This, of course, isn't the first time in American history that such a discovery has been made. It is central to the progressive tradition which, since the writing of the Constitution, was expressed as early as the anti-federalists, as well as by the Jacksonians, the Progressive party later in the nineteenth century and, perhaps in its most revolutionary manifestation during the New Deal. Within this purview, the sixties were decisively an engagement in the world which dramatically disclosed that the gates to the Castle could be pried open—a bit.

Surpassing this, however, the 1960s also witnessed a gradually dawning awareness that to once again search out the initial cracks in the technocratic fortress wasn't adequate for a progressive politics: that the parameters and texture of power were much more indirect and tricky to apprehend and resist than we thought. Corporatist ascendancy has never been an imposition on the many. It is, instead, a statement of the values, attitudes, and derivative idea of opportunity as lucre to which we are all carefully trained and habitually attached. And it is only this realization about our tyranny over ourselves which can plausibly lead to the understanding that the countervailing values, attitudes, and essential economic position integral to the organization of modern science becomes an incontrovertible contradiction, encouraging an egalitarian ethos and an actual pluralism of power and authority which infiltrate the dominance of a technological and corporatist consciousness—as well as the policies which must follow from this dominance.

That such an awareness takes a while to find public effect goes without saying. Yet the process of comprehending the subtle dimensions of power and authority, and their connection to opportunity, is invariably slow and, indeed, frustrating. As Niels Bohr proposed, complementarity in the nature of existence is a condition wherein the contradiction hides not only from human perception, but from itself.

But to be engaged in the world is exactly to stumble ahead. And this is what we have done so far. Within this engagement we try to discover ourselves by constructing categories that serve our convenience and what may be our limited capacity to detect the resonating tones of historical change. And, even if the impulse behind this dialectical stumbling—which is the motion of human history—can't be fully ascertained, we must appreciate the fact that our attempt to scientifically perceive it constitutes a profoundly democratic act.

This is because revolution is ultimately nothing but a reflection of human engagement, both within the self and in a larger universe. It is a phenomenon that is animated by the ambition to rationally confront an empirically discernible reality and, more overtly, by compatible action in the public space which, as Arendt suggests, is all that ever causes the inevitable not to happen.[4] Revolution is the opportunity to surpass illusion and move to a freer engagement with the sensory world: to seek power in and through a material milieu, and through the dilemmas and contradictions that compose it and that complicate our efforts to address it. This is an opportunity that stimulates a more inclusive consciousness of the commonalities of power that permeate the history of the species, and a corresponding ability to find integrated and productive purpose within the growing equality of a planetary environment that we increasingly know must be shared.

To be sure, as the Nazi and fascist episodes demonstrate, a technocratic nation can turn away from the egalitarian vector of science in favor of a regressive, elitist, and nationalistic Romanticism: a penchant, once loose, that will virtually poison the rational roots of modernity. Still, at least to this point, the West continues to be a house of reason which, when fused with a commitment to the equality of empirical verification, is translated into a house of science. In the final analysis, this is all we have—all that the human need for the fuller intention and variation that evolves from the power of freedom can rely on in regard to a species which, whatever the enchantments and exuberances of the moment, historically gravitates toward the most convincing pronouncements about a stubbornly material existence.

This is a process that becomes inescapably vivid in an age when status and power are patently associated with the achievements of organized science. It is a time in which an intransigent liberal consciousness reacts against the broader egalitarian claim it historically implies by decrying the scientific endeavor it once applauded, increasingly anxious to refute that unity of science and democracy which emanates from the nuances of dialectical tension and political disputation. Hence, as scientific action becomes more pivotal to public policy, those who speak for a traditional liberalism confuse others, and often themselves, by insidiously denigrating further theoretical ventures within science even as they aggrandize technology, a posture, if maintained long enough, which endemically brings with it the tangible basis of fascism.

But such are the convolutions of history—exceeding by far the solace of those comforting references and responses of generational conditioning. While we are momentarily preoccupied with the present Thermidor, it is strictly the concordance of opposites within a corporatist order—the generic concurrence of science and technology—which energizes our inclinations to reach succeeding levels of the intensifying pluralism that announces the power and authority of revolutionary expression. Indeed, this was precisely the prelude to the 1960s.

So we wait for the movement to stir. And, conceivably, to move once more. Yet motion is invariable, however unnoticed most of the time, and the need for engagement in the world is consistently projected into a yearning for civic power and freedom; two sides of the same coin; an ardent pressure for an egalitarian community grounded in a different kind of opportunity that won't simply go away.[5] Within this is the force behind those subtle refrains of the human experience, inducing a more egalitarian role in a formulation of reality that accords with the cosmological, epistemological, and ethical stipulations of the scientific outlook. And, with notable rapidity, the attempt to comprehend in a manner more fully compatible with an augmented empirical glimpse into the more elusive domains of human need changes the values and attitudes of populations, invigorating a consciousness which must seek a less stunted version of opportunity than that which appears to incessantly prevail.

Nonetheless, now imbued with the lifestyle "pluralism" of the "postmodernist" vogue, which neutralizes any effort to find theoretical insight through the assertion that nothing is more important than anything else, this remains a country which chases the immediate in the name of the main chance—wherein the pleasures of the deference and status which flow from consumption are fleeting and the gratification of true validation avoids the general grasp. Much has been said about this. It is conclusively the substance of the progressive critique. However, within the consequent perception there is no theory of history and, thus, no coherence.

What is required is a larger scheme. In a civilization becoming scientific, this has to be a scheme available to the evidence of the senses. It must incorporate an idea of history incisive enough to afford intelligibility in a land wherein attention to memory possesses no currency and which, therefore, is hardly burdened with clues about the dialectical nature of the revolutionary force that is the very determinant of its being. Still, only from this perspective can we obtain a hint of our personal and systemic selves.

As the population grudgingly admits that things aren't as they are supposed to be, it becomes clear that "American exceptionalism" must break with its reflexive attachment to "free" markets and finally come to grips with the transcending necessities of power in a postindustrial epoch. Camouflaged by the mirage of "entrepreneurial opportunity," these instill the paramount paradox wherein, as might be expected, the sweep of the controlling force is moving in two directions at the same moment: into a corporatist suzerainty on one hand and toward a more egalitarian constellation of power and authority on the other.

Here is a force that demands a new dream. But a new dream involves a dramatic shift in the sanitized interpretation about where we've been and of the ramifying probabilities of our present politics. The capacity of a sophisticated technology to eliminate a perennial material scarcity and to introduce an economics of abundance neutralizes even the vestiges of the commercial pluralism of a liberal market which, more and more explicitly, must function within the constrictions of technobureaucratic concerns. The postindustrial era, with organized labor absorbed into an implicit loyalty to multinational business interests, simultaneously ensures that effective opposition to established power can no longer be located within a dialectical discord of bourgeoisie and proletariat. Yet America is now, in fact, subsumed by a volatile struggle for opportunity and power; one that surges from a material force in the throes of contradiction; propelling a global tension between a mentality that supports the action of a technocratic authoritarianism and the mentality of an egalitarian pluralism which hides within the opposing action and labor of contemporary science. Such is the pervading expression of a tension that always attends those instruments of production which historically infuse the human situation and delineate the scope of its political possibilities.

The movement of the sixties touched the edges of revolution to the degree that it assaulted the edges of power. This is why, regardless of the predictable regression it caused, many of the successes of that decade have come to possess a lasting quality. However, much as the accepted theories of the 1960s missed the point that the elitism of a capitalist consciousness can't tolerate political equality, so they ignored the productive energies which are the formative foundation of the American order. In this, they were myopic about the ideological adhesive which justifies power and authority in a liberal system. That they accordingly failed to arrive at a sufficiently acute focus on the controlling idea of opportunity and its inherent connection to the revolutionary process shouldn't be surprising.

This is because the crucial factor of production is no longer capital accumulation with its corollary conception of the free market as opportunity. Along with technical virtuosity, it is the opportunity for science, as Jefferson expounded,[6] which must be released by the enhancement of liberty. And it is science, in its political extrapolation, which comprises the material catalyst of democracy and of the expanded freedom which accompanies any further distribution of civic authority. Amidst the present disarray, the center moves, as it always does. And within the resulting cacophony of control and diversity—within the quest for countervailing power—technology magnifies the impact of both parties to the struggle. But this isn't true of science, which exclusively carries into the polis the complex symphony of a more egalitarian pluralism.

While scientific enterprise replaces large capital investment as the great adventure of our century, it is precisely the force of science and technology in combination, and the clash of values, organization, and power this sets in motion—a force in opposition to itself—which imposes a more advanced understanding upon the meaning of opportunity for America. Beyond all else, this is what the movement of the 1960s must convey to our generation and, with far greater certainty, will convey to the generations that follow. It is only this which can eventually yield a more enlightened and humane comprehension of the insistent contours of revolution.

"The thrill is gone?"

Seems like we heard that one before.

Appendix: "Elite" and "Social Class" as Conceptual Frameworks

"Elite," "elitist," "elitism," and "elite theory" all refer to special claims to rule, presumably in the public interest, whether the relevant arena is thought of as "political" or not. But, while often confused for each other, these terms are really not interchangeable, a point which could probably stand a bit of clarification here.

The word "elite" simply denotes "the few," or "the one," who are considered qualified or, at least, most qualified, to govern, in whatever realm and whatever the foundation of the claim. By extension, in the context, for instance, of race, ethnicity, religion, or nationality it often can be appropriately applied to "the many." However, the issue soon becomes more complex.

An "elitist" advocates "elitism." Such a view invariably argues, overtly or implicitly, that a certain one, few, or many, should govern because he, she, or they possess an inborn capacity which is not present in other people or, more characteristically, not present to the degree required for right rule. The nature of this alleged capacity varies, depending upon the advocate or the tradition within which the advocation occurs. Yet, whatever the asserted "capacity" may be, the elitist will nearly always insist that it has to be nurtured and educated and, thereby, transformed into an "ability," a perspective which must infer that ability is the actualization of capacity. Accordingly, those who arrive in the world without the necessary capacity—or with too little of it—can never attain the ability to govern or, quite typically, to even share in governing, and no amount of attempted cultivation can change this.

"Elite theory" is quite another matter, as is the "elite theorist" who advances it. A theory represents an effort to explain, and an elite theory affirms that whoever, in fact, rules is, or are, perceived as possessing a special ability to do so by, at a minimum, a critical mass of those who are being ruled. Acceptance of this kind could indicate a concurrence within a population about a particular brand of elitism, or it might merely express an agreement that, among people who are considered equal, one—a few—or even the many—but not all—have developed a qualifying expertise.

An elite theory may be articulated by an elitist, or by an egalitarian who, for whatever reasons, is convinced of the necessity of elite rule, or from myriad other perspectives, but these concerns have no relevance to the theory *as a theory*. Moreover, the theorist could find that authority is held by a single elite (i.e., in part, Gaetano Mosca, *The Ruling Class: Elementi Di Scienza Politica*, ed. and rev., with an intro. by Arthur Livingston, trans. by Hannah D. Kahn [New York: McGraw-Hill Book Co., 1939], especially pp. 134 and 146 and passim); by competing elites (i.e., Harold D. Lasswell, *Politics: Who Gets What, When, How* [New York: Peter Smith, 1950]); by circulating elites (i.e., Vilfredo Pareto, *The Rise and Fall of the Elites: An Application of Theoretical Sociology*, with an intro. by Hans L. Zetterberg [Totowa, NJ: The Bedminster Press, 1968], especially chap. 3, "The Decline of the Old Elite," pp. 59–71, and chap. 4, "The Rise of the New Elite," pp. 72–89 and passim, and Vilfredo Pareto, *The Transformation of Democracy*, ed. with an intro. by Charles H. Powers, trans. by Renata Girola [New Brunswick, NJ: Transaction Books, 1984], especially chap. 3, "The Plutocratic Cycle," pp. 55–62 and passim); or by a gradation of elites (i.e., Gabriel A. Almond, *The American People and Foreign Policy* [New York: Frederick A. Praeger, Publishers, 1960], especially chap. 1, "World Leadership and Human Material," pp. 3–10, and, in particular, 10, and chap. 7, "The Elites and Foreign Policy," pp. 136–157 and passim, and, in particular, "Types of Foreign Policy Elites," pp. 139–143). There are, of course, other possible variations on the theme of elite theory, although these are probably the essential formulations.

Within the elite systems being theorized about, upward and

downward mobility must be discerned as volatile because where people find themselves within the structure is purportedly determined by their individual capacities and, finally, abilities. In the United States, for example, the liberal idea of "equal opportunity" is the central ideological expression of such a perceptual reality.

By comparison, snobbery, which may be annoying to some, is not significant to claims about power and authority. It is best understood as a quirk of the personality not necessarily rooted in a consistent certainty of an intrinsically superior capacity to govern.

The phenomenon of upward and downward mobility leads to the core difference between "elite systems" and "social-class systems." Strictly speaking, a "class" is simply a category. However, in modern sociological analysis, social class means much more. Plainly, elite systems and social-class systems are hierarchical in form: both represent "top-down" or "vertical" arrangements of power and authority—in contrast to "democratic systems," which are "across-the-board" or "horizontal"—or to reasonably developed systems of pluralism which, while not democratic, are far more horizontal than those predicated upon elite or social-class domination. Yet, unlike elite systems, upward and downward mobility within social-class systems is, by definition, comparatively gradual, and not achievable within the lifetime of any one person but, depending upon the specific system, only within that of several generations or more. This is because the controlling factor in a social-class system is not personal capacity and ability. It is, instead, the social status of the family that a person is born into, and it is only as members of their families that people move up or down in reference to the prevailing configurations of power and authority.

Relatively slow upward and downward mobility is a fundamental feature of social-class systems. In this sense, Marx and Engels are elite theorists and not class theorists, regardless of their contention that the location of people within the hierarchy of power and authority is an expression of their economic role, since this role can change dramatically within the lifetime of any particular person, and might do so, rapidly, any number of times.

Social-class systems can be conceived of as "functional" (i.e., Karl Marx and Frederick Engels, *Manifesto of the Communist Party*, authorized English trans., ed. and annotated by Frederick Engels [New York: International Publishers, 1948], especially Part I, "Bourgeois and Proletarians," pp. 9–21 and passim), even though, as indicated, Marx and Engels are really proposing an elite theory, or as "relational" (i.e., W. Lloyd Warner and Paul S. Lunt, *The Social Life of a Modern Community*, in W. Lloyd Warner, Yankee City Series, 6 vols. [New Haven: Yale University Press, 1941], vol. 1), wherein the position of each social class is determined by its relationship to other social classes which, in turn, are also so determined. Nevertheless, the crucial importance of family affiliation pertains whether a social class is viewed as functional or defined by its relationship to other social classes, whatever the basis, or bases, of this relationship may be (i.e., family income).

In addition, social classes can be identified by an "objective" criterion, or criteria, or wherein the theorist decides who belongs to what social class (i.e., Marx and Engels, *Manifesto of the Communist Party*), noting, once again, that what is really being referred to, in this instance, are elites; by a "subjective" criterion, or criteria, wherein those being studied place themselves into the social class to which they think they belong (i.e., Warner and Lunt, *Social Life of a Modern Community*); or, in a variation of the subjective approach, by a "reputational" criterion, or criteria, wherein people are considered to be members of a specific social class according to their reputation in this regard with others (i.e., Floyd Hunter, *Top Leadership U.S.A.* [Chapel Hill, NC: The University of North Carolina Press, 1959], especially Part I, "Finding the Leaders," pp. 1–112). Usually, the objective and functional approaches are combined (i.e., Marx and Engels, *Manifesto of the Communist Party*), as are the subjective and relational approaches (i.e., Warner and Lunt, *Social Life of a Modern Community*), although an interesting attempt to fuse the subjective and functional approaches is found in W. Lloyd Warner, with the collaboration of Wilfrid C. Bailey, Arch Cooper, Walter Eaton, A.B. Hollingshead, Carson McGuire, Marchia Meeker, Bernie Newgarten, Joseph Rosenstein, Evon Z. Vogt, Jr., and Donald Wray, *Democracy in Jonesville: A Study of Quality and Inequality*, The Academy Library (New York: Harper and Row, Publishers, Harper Torchbooks, 1949), especially chap. 2, "Status in the Democracy of Jonesville," pp. 22–34. As with elite theories, there are further feasible variations on the theme of social-class theory.

None of this, it might be mentioned, has anything to do with acting with, or having, "class," despite the fact that attempts can be, and clearly have been, made to connect such behavior to inclusion within a certain social class.

Finally, a "social-caste system," predicated as it is upon family membership, is really a social-class system within which no upward or downward mobility actually exists.

The distinction between elites and social classes becomes more complicated when a social-class analysis incorporates elites—predicated upon the supposed capacities and abilities of their members—which actually govern within a social-class, or social-caste, system while subject to the limitations mandated by the larger system (i.e., Paul M. Sweezy, "The American Ruling Class," Part I, *Monthly Review: An Independent Socialist Magazine*, May 1951, pp. 10–17, and Paul M. Sweezy, "The American Ruling Class," Part II, ibid., June 1951, pp. 58–64, and, especially, "Divisions and Conflicts within the Ruling Class," Part II, pp. 63–64, also available in Paul M. Sweezy, chap. 9, "The American Ruling Class," Part I, in *The Present as History: Essays and Reviews on Capitalism and Socialism* [New York: Monthly Review Press, 1953], pp. 120–129, and Paul M.

Sweezy, "The American Ruling Class," Part II, in ibid., pp. 129–138, and, especially, "How the Ruling Class Rules," pp. 134–138).

In addition, there is the problem of social classes that do not fit into the class structure as elaborated by the theorist as, for example, "the *nouveau riche*" (Sweezy, "American Ruling Class," Part I, *Monthly Review*, May, 1951, p. 13 and passim, and Sweezy, chap. 9, "American Ruling Class," Part I, in *Present as History*, p. 124 and passim), or "the *nouveaux riches*" (Part II, *Monthly Review*, p. 58 and passim, and Part II, in *Present as History*, p. 130 and passim); "the middle class," which can be viewed as "a collection of fringes" (Part I, *Monthly Review*, p. 16 and passim, and Part I, in *Present as History*, p. 129 and passim), of "the ruling class above it and . . . the working class below it" (Part I, *Monthly Review*, p. 16 and passim, and Part I, in *Present as History*, p. 129 and passim); and "declassed elements" (Part I, *Monthly Review*, p. 15 and passim, and Part I, in *Present as History*, p. 126 and passim).

Extremely useful in reference to identifying the differences between elites and social classes is Paul M. Sweezy, "Power Elite or Ruling Class?," review of *The Power Elite* by C. Wright Mills, *Monthly Review: An Independent Socialist Magazine*, September 1956, pp. 138–150.

Fundamentally, the conception of "elite" emphasizes the supposed capacities and abilities of the individual while that of "social class" emphasizes the social structure itself.

Notes

Introduction

1. José Ortega y Gasset, "The Sunset of Revolution," in José Ortega y Gasset, *The Modern Theme*, trans. by James Cleugh, with an intro. by José Ferrater Mora, The Academy Library (New York: Harper and Row, Publishers, Harper Torchbooks, 1961), pp. 99–131. Or, maybe somewhat less profoundly, José Ortega y Gasset, *The Revolt of the Masses*, authorized translation from the Spanish (New York: W. W. Norton and Co., 1932), presumably a portrayal of the manifestations of this revolution in the twentieth century. For an earlier and simpler version of this, cf., Gustave Le Bon, *The Crowd: A Study of the Popular Mind*, with a new intro. by Robert K. Merton (New York: The Viking Press, 1960).

2. Albert Camus, *The Rebel: An Essay on Man in Revolt*, with a Foreword by Sir Herbert Read, a rev. and complete trans. of *L'Homme Révolté* by Anthony Bower (New York: Random House, Vintage Books, 1956), especially Part Three, "Historical Rebellion," pp. 105–252, and, in particular, "Rebellion and Revolution," pp. 246–252.

3. Erich Fromm, "The Revolutionary Character," in Erich Fromm, The Dogma of Christ: And Other Essays on Religion, *Psychology and Culture* (New York: Doubleday and Co., Anchor Books, 1966), pp. 149–171.

4. Samuel P. Huntington, *Political Order in Changing Societies*, Henry L. Stimson Lectures, in part (New Haven: Yale University Press, 1968), pp. 264, 266, 264, and 265. As Huntington indicates, the interior quotation is from Carl Joachim Friedrich, *Man and His Government: An Empirical Theory of Politics* (New York: McGraw-Hill Book Co., 1963), p. 644, and, more generally, chap. 34, "Resistance and Revolution," pp. 634–656.

In this regard, it might be useful to consider what is meant by phrases like the "total destruction of the established system," James C. Davies, "The J-Curve of Rising and Declining Satisfactions as a Cause of Some Great Revolutions and a Contained Rebellion," in Hugh Davis Graham and Ted Robert Gurr (eds.), *The History of Violence in America: Historical and Comparative Perspectives*, with a special intro. by John Herbes, A Report Submitted to the National Commission on the Causes and Prevention of Violence, A New York Times Book (New York: Frederick A. Praeger, Publishers, 1969), p. 711.

5. Much of this critique of Huntington is replicated from Paul N. Goldstene, "Veblen's Theory of Value and the Problem of Revolution," a symposium with John Patrick Diggins, Michael W. Hughey and Arthur J. Vidich, Paul N. Goldstene, and Clare Virginia Eby, on *Thorstein Veblen and His Crit-*

111

ics, *1891–1963: Conservative, Liberal, and Radical Perspectives*, by Rick Tilman, in *International Journal of Politics, Culture and Society*, Summer, 1993, pp. 507–520, and, especially, 508–510.

6. Theda Skocpol, *States and Social Revolutions: A Comparative Analysis of France, Russia, and China* (New York: Cambridge University Press, 1989), especially chap. 1, "Introduction: Exploring Social Revolutions: Alternatives to Existing Theories," pp. 1–43, and "Conclusion," pp. 284–293, and, in particular, 19 and passim.

7. Huntington, *Political Order in Changing Societies*, p. 32 and passim, and, especially, 39. Crane Brinton, *The Anatomy of Revolution*, rev. and expanded ed. (New York: Random House, Vintage Books, 1965), p. 39 and passim, and, especially, 45, 46, and 59, wherein the word "elite" is not employed but is subsumed into the conception of "class," p. 50 and passim, and, in particular, 50–52. Thus, "if we avoid the narrow economic connotations of the term, we may call these groups classes . . . we may even speak of class struggles," ibid., p. 50. To be sure, this is predicated upon a simplistic understanding of social classes as Marx conceives of them, an analysis which is actually addressed to his greater concern about the emergence of consciousness in human history. Charles Tilly, "Does Modernization Breed Revolution?," *Comparative Politics*, April 1973, pp. 425–447, and, especially, 436–437. Ted Robert Gurr, *Why Men Rebel*, published for the Center of International Studies, Princeton University (Princeton, NJ: Princeton University Press, 1970), p. 13 and passim, and, more fully, chap. 2, "Relative Deprivation and the Impetus to Violence," pp. 22–58, and chap. 3, "The Intensity and Scope of Relative Deprivation," pp. 59–91. Regarding the revolutionary role of elites, cf., "the capacity of a political system to satisfy the participatory value expectations of those who desire high levels of power, the elite aspirants, is a function of the ratio between the number of elite aspirants and the number of elite positions, weighted by the frequency of change in incumbents," ibid., p. 144. In addition, cf., ibid., pp. 136–137, 144–154 (especially 151–154), 163–164, 195–196, 211–218, 253–254, 260–272 (especially 262–267), 276–279, 283–284, 291–296, 336–338, and 340, although Gurr often uses "dissidents," p. 212 and passim, as an equivalent for members of an emerging "elite," p. 144 and passim. It might be noted that, beyond what Gurr contends about relative deprivation, it is annoyingly difficult to be specific about his argument because it is habitually expressed through the contentions of others. Consequently, his position on many essential issues must generally be derived through inference and even implication.

Also, cf., Chalmers Johnson, *Revolutionary Change*, 2nd ed. (Stanford, CA: Stanford University Press, 1982), especially chap. 2, "The Social System: Coercion and Values," pp. 16–40, and, in particular, 38–39 and 183.

Johnson, ibid., pp. 1 and passim, 61, and chap. 4, "The Disequilibrated Social System," pp. 61–90 and passim, shares the view of Gurr, *Why Men*

Rebel, p. 50 and passim, and 153 and passim; Huntington, *Political Order in Changing Societies,* p. 264 and passim; Skocpol, *States and Social Revolutions,* p. 4 and passim; and, at least by inference, Tilly, "Does Modernization Breed Revolution?," pp. 426–427, that a revolution involves a violent and rapid transformation in the core values of a social system. Such is a claim which actually renders revolutions impossible because the controlling values of a society never change rapidly, even after a successful seizure of political authority, cf., Brinton, *Anatomy of Revolution,* p. 6 and passim, and, perhaps as a logical contradiction, suggested in Tilly, "Does Modernization Breed Revolution?," pp. 433–434. In any event, this is unlikely to be disturbing to Gurr, Johnson and, in relationship to Western countries, Huntington, who are far more concerned with perceived threats to systemic maintenance than with the substance of revolution.

8. For the relevance of elites to revolutions, see Skocpol, *States and Social Revolutions,* pp. 13–14 and passim, although, like Brinton, the idea of "class," p. xii and passim, is used by Skocpol in a manner which incorporates elites. On revolutions "from below," see ibid., p. 4 and passim, xv and passim, and, especially, 33.

9. Brinton, *Anatomy of Revolution,* chap. 9, "A Summary of the Work of Revolutions," pp. 237–264, and, in particular, 246 and 260.

10. Huntington, *Political Order in Changing Societies,* although Huntington refers to this as "modernization," thus, "more precisely, revolution is characteristic of modernization," p. 264.

11. Skocpol, *States and Social Revolutions,* p. 18 and passim, and, especially, 292–293.

12. Brinton, *Anatomy of Revolution,* p. 28 and passim, and, in particular, 34.

13. Theodore J. Lowi, "The State in Political Science: How We Become What We Study," *American Political Science Review,* March 1992, pp. 1–7, especially 5–6.

14. Erich Fromm, *The Anatomy of Human Destructiveness* (New York: Holt, Rinehart and Winston, 1973), p. 261.

15. Huntington, *Political Order in Changing Societies,* pp. 334–343 and passim. Accordingly, for instance, "Marxism" is "a theory of social evolution" and "Leninism" is "a theory of political action," ibid., p. 337. In reference to this distinction by Huntington, cf., Goldstene, "Veblen's Theory of Value and the Problem of Revolution," p. 509.

16. Ibid., p. 268.

17. I thought this was from Skocpol, *States and Social Revolutions,* and that I simply could not locate the appropriate page. However, my letter of inquiry about this to Professor Skocpol of October 24, 1994 and her note in response of October 31, 1994 indicate that it must have been written by someone else. I have no idea who this might be, but the phrase is useful while I remain convinced that it is not of my invention.

18. Hannah Arendt, *On Revolution* (New York: The Viking Press, A Viking Compass Book, 1963).

19. David Easton, *The Political System: An Inquiry into the State of Political Science* (New York: Alfred A. Knopf, 1964). The contentions made here about science are similar to those made more specifically in reference to political science in ibid., chap. 2, "The Condition of American Political Science," pp. 37–63, especially section 3, "The Role of Theory," pp. 52–63, chap. 3, "Conceptions of Science and Theory in Empirical Research," pp. 64–89, and, well summarized, 63.

This view of the scientific perspective will probably not be met with approval by more than a few in the social sciences. Perhaps the only useful response to those who react in this manner is to urge them to read the writings of many of those who have made major theoretical contributions to the natural sciences.

20. Cf., Thomas S. Kuhn, *The Structure of Scientific Revolutions*, 2nd ed. enlarged, International Encyclopedia of Unified Science (Chicago: The University of Chicago Press, 1975), vol. 2, no. 2, wherein it is argued that "ambiguities," p. 34 and passim, and "anomalies," p. 6 and passim, within an accepted scientific "paradigm," p. ix and passim, sometimes lead to "paradigm changes," p. 115 and passim, or "a . . . paradigm shift," p. 119 and passim. Cf., especially, ibid., chap. 6, "Anomaly and the Emergence of Scientific Discoveries," pp. 52–65, and chap. 7, "Crisis and the Emergence of Scientific Theories," pp. 66–76.

21. John Kenneth Galbraith, *The Affluent Society*, The Riverside Press, Cambridge (Boston: Houghton Mifflin Co., 1958), p. 9 and passim, and, more fully, chap. 2, "The Concept of the Conventional Wisdom," pp. 7–20 and passim.

22. Perhaps it is more accurate to refer to this as "person-specific (*not* 'personal')," as insisted upon in Clifford Geertz, *Works and Lives: The Anthropologist as Author*, The Harry Camp Lectures at Stanford University (Stanford, CA: Stanford University Press, 1988), p. 6 and passim. It is pertinent to note that the same phenomenon in science is at times referred to as "personal knowledge," cf., Michael Polanyi, *Personal Knowledge: Towards a Post-Critical Philosophy* (Chicago: The University of Chicago Press, 1962), p. vii and passim, capitalized for emphasis in the original in its first usage. Thus, "I start by rejecting the ideal of scientific detachment. In the exact sciences, this false ideal is perhaps harmless, for it is in fact disregarded there by scientists. But we shall see that it exercises a destructive influence in biology, psychology and sociology, and falsifies our whole outlook far beyond the domain of science," ibid, p. vii, although what is excluded from "the domain of science" is not made clear.

23. John Dunn, *Modern Revolutions: An Introduction to the Analysis of a Political Phenomenon*, 2nd ed. (Cambridge, England: Cambridge University Press, 1989), pp. 2 and 1–2.

Chapter 1

1. Cf., Georg Simmel, *On Individuality and Social Forms: Selected Writings*, ed. with an intro. by Donald N. Levine, The Heritage of Sociology Series, ed. by Morris Janowitz (Chicago: The University of Chicago Press, 1971), p. xv and passim, and, especially, chap. 6, "Forms Versus Life Process: The Dialectic of Change," pp. 349–393.

2. With, I suppose, apologies to T.S. Eliot, "The Hollow Men, 1925," in T.S. Eliot, *Collected Poems: 1909–1962* (San Diego: Harcourt Brace Jovanovich, Publishers, 1970), pp. 77–82.

3. Literally, the eleventh month of the French revolutionary calendar, a word first employed to describe the beginning of the return to "normalcy" following the "fanatical" phase of the French Revolution.

4. Carl Sandburg, "The People, Yes," in Carl Sandburg, *Complete Poems* (New York: Harcourt, Brace, and Co., 1950), p. 615.

5. The political implications of this are considered more thoroughly in Paul N. Goldstene, *The Bittersweet Century: Speculations on Modern Science and American Democracy*, Chandler and Sharp Publications in Political Science, ed. by Victor Jones (Novato, CA: Chandler and Sharp Publishers, 1992), chap. 4, "Form and Process in a Liberal World," pp. 32–40.

6. C. Wright Mills, *The Power Elite* (New York: Oxford University Press, 1956), p. 25.

7. This must be attributed to Henry R. Luce, *The American Century*, with comments by Dorothy Thompson, John Chamberlain, Quincy Howe, Robert G. Spivak, and Robert W. Sherwood (New York: Farrar and Rinehart, 1941).

8. In the expressive phrase employed by Henry Steele Commager, *The Empire of Reason: How Europe Imagined and America Realized the Enlightenment* (Garden City, NY: Anchor Press, Doubleday, Anchor Books, 1978).

9. James Madison, "The Federalist," in Alexander Hamilton, John Jay, and James Madison, *The Federalist: A Commentary on the Constitution of The United States: Being a Collection of Essays Written in Support of the Constitution Agreed Upon September 17, 1787, by the Federal Convention*, no. 51, with an intro. by Edward Mead Earle, The Modern Library (New York: Random House, n.d.), p. 337.

10. C.B. Macpherson, *The Political Theory of Possessive Individualism: Hobbes to Locke* (Oxford, England: Oxford University Press, Oxford University Paperback, 1964), p. v and passim, quoted for emphasis in the original in its first usage. This is derived from "the original seventeenth-century individualism" which propounds a "conception of the individual as essentially the proprietor of his own person or capacities, owing nothing to society for them," and wherein "the individual was seen neither as a moral whole, nor as part of a larger social whole, but as an owner of himself," ibid., p. 3. In this regard, cf., C.B. Macpherson, "The Deceptive Task of Political Theory,"

The Cambridge Journal (Cambridge, England: Bowes and Bowes, June 1954), pp. 560–568, and, in particular, 564, quoted for emphasis in the original in its first usage, and C.B. Macpherson, "Natural Rights in Hobbes and Locke," 1967, in D.D. Raphael (ed.), *Political Theory and the Rights of Man* (Bloomington, IN: Indiana University Press, 1967), chap. 1, pp. 1–15, and, in particular, 13. Also available in C.B. Macpherson, Essay XI, "The Deceptive Task of Political Theory," and Essay XIII, "Natural Rights in Hobbes and Locke," in C.B. Macpherson, *Democratic Theory: Essays in Retrieval* (Oxford, England: Oxford University Press, Clarendon Press, 1973), pp. 194–203, and, in particular, 199, quoted for emphasis in the original in its first usage, in Part Two, "Related Papers on the Twentieth-Century Predicament," pp. 14–203, and pp. 224–237, and, in particular, 235, in Part Three, "Seventeenth-Century Roots of the Twentieth-Century Predicament," pp. 205–250.

11. Madison, *Federalist*, no. 48, p. 321.

Chapter 2

1. John Adams, "Discourses on Davila," in *The Works of John Adams: Second President of the United States*, with a life of the author and and illustrations by Charles Francis Adams, 10 vols. (Boston: Charles C. Little and James Brown, 1851), vol. 6, in particular, pp. 232 and, more generally, 232–235 and passim, italicized for emphasis in the original in its first usage.

2. Cf., "a belief in our extraordinary birth, outside the processes of time, has led us to think of ourselves as a nation apart, with a special destiny, the hope of all those outside America's shores," Garry Wills, *Inventing America: Jefferson's Declaration of Independence* (Garden City, NY: Doubleday and Co., 1978), p. xix. This is an excellent statement of the attitude of American exceptionalism. However, it ignores the economic ideology which is the real basis of the pluralism this position acclaims, as well as its aggressive and self-righteous influence on the foreign policy of the United States since, by stipulation, those who are party to the social contract have no obligations to those who are not, beyond making such people more like themselves.

Also cf., Philip Abbott, "Redeeming American Exceptionalism, Redeeming American Political Science: An analysis of Judith N. Shklar's Presidential Address," *The Social Science Journal: Official Journal of the Western Social Science Association* (Greenwich, CT: JAI Press, July 1995), pp. 219–234. To a lesser extent, the same proviso about the free-market basis of American exceptionalism applies here as well.

3. C.f., Paul N, Goldstene, *The Collapse of Liberal Empire: Science and Revolution in the Twentieth Century* (New Haven: Yale University Press, 1977), and Chandler and Sharp Publications in Political Science, ed. by Victor Jones (Novato, CA: Chandler and Sharp Publishers, 1980), especially Part II, "Collapse," pp. 33–87.

Chapter 3

1. A point I owe to discussions with Claire C. Goldstene.

2. Creel Froman, *The Two American Political Systems: Society, Economics, and Politics* (Englewood Cliffs, NJ: Prentice-Hall, 1984), pp. 51–52, and, more generally, chap. 3, "Corporate Wealth and Economic Power," pp. 31–49, and chap. 4, "Individual Wealth and Income," pp. 51–66 and passim.

3. Findings of a study by the Internal Revenue Service, as reported in the *San Francisco Chronicle*, August 28, 1990.

4. In 1973 the wealth distributions in the United States were 40.1 percent individuals and families, 21.7 percent government, and 37.3 percent business, Froman, *Two American Political Systems*, pp. 32–33, wherein "50 percent" of business holdings were "controlled by approximately 200 corporations, or 0.0014 of 1 percent of the 14,740,000 business enterprises in the country," p. 36, and, more generally, 33–37 and passim. Since 1973 the figure designating the corporate share has certainly become a substantially larger portion of the total.

In regard to power in the American system, however, the real issue is control of productive wealth. For a concise statement of this condition by 1967, see John Kenneth Galbraith, *The New Industrial State* (Boston: Houghton Mifflin Co., 1967), pp. 74–76, and the relevant documentation, p. 75, n. 2, 3, and 4, and 76, n. 7 and 8.

Also see an augmented version of this in John Kenneth Galbraith, *The New Industrial State*, 2nd ed., rev. (Boston: Houghton Mifflin Co., 1971), pp. 75–76, and the relevant documentation wherein the realities of economic and financial concentration are revealed to be greater than in the earlier edition, p. 75, n. 2, 3, 4, 5, and 6, and 76, n. 7 and 8.

Chapter 4

1. For empirical verification of the last point, see W. Lloyd Warner, with the collaboration of Wilfrid C. Bailey, Arch Cooper, Walter Eaton, A.B. Hollingshead, Carson McGuire, Marchia Meeker, Bernie Neugarten, Joseph Rosenstein, Evon Z. Vogt, Jr., and Donald Wray, *Democracy in Jonesville: A Study in Quality and Inequality*, The Academy Library (New York: Harper and Row, Publishers, Harper Torchbooks, 1949), especially chap. 2, "Status in the Democracy of Jonesville," pp. 22–34; also cited supra, p. 109.

A fuller development of such evidence is found in W. Lloyd Warner and Paul S. Lunt, *The Social Life of a Modern Community*, in W. Lloyd Warner, Yankee City Series, 6 vols. (New Haven: Yale University Press, 1941), vol. 1; also cited supra, p. 108.

Also see Robert S. Lynd and Helen Merrell Lynd, *Middletown: A Study in Contemporary American Culture* (New York: Harcourt, Brace and Co., 1929);

Middletown in Transition: A Study in Cultural Conflicts (New York: Harcourt, Brace and Co., 1937); and Daniel Bell, "The Background and Development of Marxian Socialism in the United States," in *Socialism and American Life*, ed. by Drew Egbert and Stow Persons, 11 vols., Princeton Studies in American Civilization (Princeton, NJ: Princeton University Press, 1952), vol. 1, pp. 213–405.

2.   Dunn, *Modern Revolutions*, p. 245 and passim.

3.   Brinton, *Anatomy of Revolution*, p. 22.

4.   The generally accepted, if somewhat-murky, formulation of this is found in Isaiah Berlin, "Two Concepts of Liberty," in Isaiah Berlin, *Four Essays on Liberty* (London: Oxford University Press, 1969), pp. 118–172, and, especially, 121–122. Much better is the distinction between "liberty" and "freedom" in Arendt, *On Revolution*, pp. 21–28, 129–130, 135, 220–221, 258–259, and 236–237, and, more generally, chap. 3, "The Pursuit of Happiness," pp. 111–137 and passim. Also, cf., Karl Marx and Frederick Engels, *The Holy Family, Or Critique of Critical Criticism: Against Bruno Bauer and Company* (1845), trans. By Richard Dixon and Clemens Dutt, in *Karl Marx, Frederick Engels: Collected Works*, 47 vols. (New York: International Publishers, 1975), vol. 4 "Marx and Engels: 1844–45," trans. By Jack Cohen, Richard Dixon, Clemens Dutt, Barbara Ruhemann, Christopher Upward, and Florence Kelly-Wischnewetzky, p. 131 and passim.

5.   Arendt, *On Revolution*, pp. 53–54 and passim, 140, and 221.

6.   Ibid., pp. 258–259.

7.   Of use here is the conception of "the 'political formula,'" Gaetano Mosca, *The Ruling Class: Elementi di Scienza Politica*, ed. and rev., with an intro. by Arthur Livingston, trans. by Hannah D. Kahn (New York: McGraw-Hill Book Co., 1939), p. 70 and passim, quoted for emphasis in the original in its first usage, through which, in one or another of its several variations, all systems are allegedly governed. Especially relevant is the contention that in allegedly democratic orders "the leaders of the governing class are the exclusive interpreters . . . of the will of the people . . . and when no other organized social forces exist apart from those which represent the principle on which sovereignty is based . . . there can be no resistance, no effective control, to restrain a natural tendency in those who stand at the head of the social order to abuse their powers," ibid., p. 134; also cited supra, p. 106. This, of course, is a classical liberal perception of the necessary consequences of any egalitarian claim, a claim which must result in "an organized minority prevailing over a disorganized majority," ibid., p. 146; also cited supra, p. 106.

8.   Arendt, *On Revolution*, pp. 226–227.

9.   Thomas Jefferson, "To Isaac H. Tiffany," Monticello, August 26, 1816, in *The Writings of Thomas Jefferson: Definitive Edition, Containing His Autobiography, On Virginia, Parliamentary Manual, Official Papers, Messages and Addresses, and Other Writings, Official and Private*, with numerous illustrations and a comprehensive analytical index, ed. by Andrew A. Lipscomb, with Albert

Ellery Bergh, 20 vols. (Washington, D.C.: The Thomas Jefferson Memorial Association of the United States, 1905), vol. 15, p. 65.

10. Archibald MacLeish, "America Was Promises (1939)," in Archibald MacLeish, *Collected Poems: 1917–1952* (Boston: Houghton Mifflin Co., The Riverside Press, Cambridge, 1952), p. 337 and passim.

Chapter 5

1. Bob Dylan, "It's Alright Ma (I'm Only Bleeding)," in Bob Dylan, *The Bob Dylan Songbook*, photographs by Chuck Stewart (New York: M. Witmark and Sons, n.d.), p. 103, punctuation adjusted.

2. V.I. Lenin, *State and Revolution* (New York: International Publishers, Little Lenin Library, 1971), especially chap. vii, "Experience of the Russian Revolutions of 1905 and 1917," p. 100, and "Postscript to the First Edition," p. 101, wherein it is noted that "it is more pleasant and useful to go through the 'experience of revolution' than to write about it."

3. Sandburg, "People, Yes," p. 577, punctuation adjusted.

4. Bertram Gross, *Friendly Fascism: The New Face of Power in America* (New York: M. Evans and Co., 1980).

5. Thomas Jefferson, "To James Madison," Fountainbleau, October 28, 1785, in *The Papers of Thomas Jefferson*, ed. by Julian P. Boyd, with Mina R. Bryan and Elizabeth L. Hutter, 25 vols. (Princeton, NJ: Princeton University Press, 1953), vol. 8, 25 February to 31 October 1785, p. 682.

6. Alan Wolfe, *The Limits of Legitimacy: Political Contradictions of Contemporary Capitalism* (New York: The Free Press, 1977), pp. 341–342.

7. John Steinbeck, "Viva Zapata!: The Screenplay," in John Steinbeck, *Zapata*, ed. and with a commentary by Robert E. Morsberger (New York: Penguin Books, 1993), p. 314.

Chapter 6

1. Samuel P. Huntington, *American Politics: The Promise of Disharmony* (Cambridge: Harvard University Press, The Belknap Press, 1981), p. 64, and, more generally, chap. 4, "Coping with the Gap," pp. 61–84 and passim.

2. Hannah Arendt, *The Human Condition*, Charles R. Walgreen Foundation Lectures (Chicago: The University of Chicago Press, 1958), pp. 132–133. Thus "mankind . . . would be free to 'consume' the whole world and to reproduce daily all things it wished to consume," ibid., p. 132.

3. Fromm, *Anatomy of Human Destructiveness*, pp. 239, and, more generally, 237–242 and passim. "The simple stimulus produces a *drive*—i.e., the person is driven by it; the activating stimulus results in a *striving*—i.e., the person is actively striving for a goal," ibid., p. 240. Accordingly, "stimuli of

the . . . simple kind, if repeated beyond a certain threshold, are no longer registered and lose their stimulating effect . . .," and "continued stimulation requires that the stimulus should either increase in intensity or change in content; a certain element of novelty is required," ibid. In contrast to this, "activating stimuli . . . do not remain 'the same'; because of the productive response to them, they are always new, always changing: the stimulated person . . . brings the stimuli to life and changes them by always discovering new aspects in them," ibid. They involve "a mutual relationship, not . . . mechanical one-way relations," ibid.

It is relevant to mention that more money is spent on advertising than on any other industry within modern "capitalist" systems, or, indeed, on all formal education, and that, "on the whole, advertising rests upon the stimulation of socially produced desires," ibid., p. 241. Thus "contemporary life in industrial societies operates almost entirely with such simple stimuli . . . mediated through movies, television, radio, newspapers, magazines, and the commodity market," ibid., pp. 240–241.

4. George Katsiaficas, *The Imagination of the New Left: A Global Analysis of 1968* (Boston: South End Press, 1987), p. 5.

5. As opposed to Romanticism, and even to Rationalism, in reference to considerations of cosmology and epistemology. This is the central argument about Jefferson in Wills, *Inventing America*, especially pp. xxii–xxiv, Part Two, "A Scientific Paper," pp. 91–164, Part Three, "A Moral Paper," pp. 165–255, and "Epilogue," pp. 363–369. Actually, this perspective on Jefferson is more directly stated in Garry Wills, *Lincoln at Gettysburg: The Words That Remade America* (New York: Simon and Schuster, A Touchstone Book, 1992), p. 103.

6. Sandburg, "People, Yes," p. 576.

Chapter 7

1. Probably the earliest formulation of this condition is the depiction of the United States as "a permanent war-preparations economy," Paul M. Sweezy, "The American Economy and the Threat of War," *Monthly Review: An Independent Socialist Magazine*, November 1950, p. 340 and passim.

Such, of course, is a system which could also be thought of as a "garrison state," Harold D. Lasswell, "The Garrison State," *The American Journal of Sociology*, January 1941, p. 456 and passim; a "Warfare State," Fred J. Cook, *The Warfare State*, with a Foreword by Bertrand Russell (New York: The Macmillan Co., 1962), p. 19 and passim, capitalized in the original for emphasis throughout; or, by extrapolation, and in slightly less assertive tones, a "national security state," Peter Schrag, *The End of the American Future* (New York: Simon and Schuster, 1973), p. 298 and passim; or, perhaps, a "national-defense state," James Fallows, *National Defense* (New York: Random House, 1981), but none of these designations really convey the considerations of political economy which are crucial to the present situation, and which the first formulation articulates.

2. Cf., Neal D. Houghton (ed.), *Struggle Against History: U.S. Foreign Policy in an Age of Revolution*, with an intro. by Arnold J. Toynbee (New York: Simon and Schuster, A Clarion Book, 1968).

3. Samuel P. Huntington, chap. 3, "The United States," in Michael Crozier, Samuel P. Huntington, and Joji Watanuki, *The Crisis of Democracy: Report on the Governability of Democracies to the Trilateral Commission* (New York: New York University Press, 1975), pp. 59–118, and, especially, 63. Not surprisingly, Huntington insists that "the effective operation of a democratic political system usually requires some measure of apathy and noninvolvement on the part of some individuals and groups," ibid., p. 114, a strange understanding of "democratic" which is, nonetheless, extremely popular in contemporary liberal systems, usually in the guise of "constitutional democracy," p. 63 and passim. Cf., this ideological inclination in Mosca, *Ruling Class*, pp. 134 and 146, cited supra, p. 118, n. 7, and passim.

Huntington's perspective on the actual purpose of a constitutional order, ibid., p. 63 and passim, is remarkably similar to the perceptions of certain of the more egalitarian critics of the United States Constitution, cf., Charles A. Beard, *An Economic Interpretation of the Constitution of the United States*, with new intro. (New York: The Macmillan Co., 1960), and J. Allen Smith, *The Spirit of American Government*, ed. by Cushing Strout, The John Harvard Library (Cambridge: Harvard University Press, The Belknap Press, 1965). In reference to the attempt to maintain the established system of power through the incorporation of a commercial elitism into the American constitutional argument, all three are correct. Also, cf., Arendt, *On Revolution*, pp. 226–227, cited supra, p. 118, n. 8, and 232–234 and passim.

4. Huntington, "The United States," in Crozier, Huntington, and Watanuki, *Crisis of Democracy*, p. 102 and passim, and, more generally, section IV, "The Democratic Distemper: Consequences," pp. 102–106, and section V, "The Democratic Distemper: Causes," pp. 106–113 and passim. This is concurrently labeled as a "democratic surge," ibid., p. 60, and "an excess of democracy," p. 113.

The incomes policy is implicit throughout, but is expressed most overtly, ibid., p. 115.

5. Cf., ibid. The result of what was proposed had to be an increase in the depressionary tendencies of the economy. Interestingly, an argument opposed to these policies is found in Appendix I: "Discussion of Study During Plenary Meeting of the Trilateral Commission, Kyoto, May 31, 1975," ibid., pp. 173–203, especially Part B, "Excerpts of Remarks by Rolf Dahrendorf on the Governability Study," pp. 188–195 and, in particular, 192 and 194. Also, cf., Appendix II "Canadian Perspectives on the Governability of Democracies, Discussion in Montreal," ibid., May 16, 1975, pp. 203–209.

For excellent depictions of the depressionary effects of policies which work to concentrate wealth for, presumably, purposes of investment, see Arthur M. Schlesinger, Jr., *The Crisis of the Old Order: 1919–1933*, The Age of Roosevelt (Boston: Houghton Mifflin Co., The Riverside Press, Cambridge, 1957), and John Kenneth Galbraith, *The Great Crash: 1929*, 2nd ed., with a new intro. by the author (Boston: Houghton Mifflin Co., The Riverside Press, Cambridge, 1961), a volume which encourages readers to laugh their way through the Great Depression, and herein recommended for those disposed to seize such an opportunity.

6. On the relationship between a certain level of material comfort and political involvement, cf., Hans J. Morgenthau, *Scientific Man vs. Power Politics* (Chicago: The University of Chicago Press, Midway Reprint, 1974), p. 193.

7. Thorstein Veblen, *The Theory of the Leisure Class: An Economic Study of Institutions*, with a Foreword by Stuart Chase, The Modern Library (New York: Random House, 1934), p. 33 and passim, and Thorstein Veblen, *The Instinct of Workmanship and the State of the Industrial Arts*, with an intro. by Dr. Joseph Dorfman (New York: Augustus M. Kelley, Bookseller, 1964), p. 27 and passim, quoted for emphasis in the original in its first usage, and, more generally, chap. 1, "The Instinct of Workmanship: Introductory," pp. 1–37.

8. Rick Tilman, *C. Wright Mills: A Native Radical and His American Intellectual Roots* (University Park, PA: The Pennsylvania University Press, 1984), pp. 74 and 75, first quotation from C. Wright Mills, "Work Milieu and Social Structure," Address to the Mental Health Society of Northern California, Asilomar, California, March 13, 1954.

9. Aside from the works of Jefferson, one of the rare attempts by an American writer to deal with the political implications of the prevailing idea of opportunity in the United States, as well as with its relationship to the democratic position, is found in John H. Schaar, chap. 13, "Equality of Opportunity and Beyond," in *Nomos*, ed. by J. Roland Pennock and John W. Chapman, 18 vols., Yearbook of the American Society for Legal and Political Philosophy (New York: Atherton Press, 1967), no. 9, *Equality*, pp. 228–249.

10. Primarily, of course, Plato and Aristotle or, perhaps, for example, in its more contemporary expression, Allan Bloom, *The Closing of the American Mind: How Higher Education Has Failed Democracy and Impoverished the Souls of Today's Students*, with a Foreword by Saul Bellow (New York: Simon and Schuster, 1987).

11. On this, cf., Paul M. Sweezy, "The American Ruling Class," Part I, *Monthly Review: An Independent Socialist Magazine*, May 1951, pp. 10–17, and Paul M. Sweezy, "The American Ruling Class," Part II, ibid., June 1951, pp. 58–64, especially the discussion of "the *nouveau riche*," Part I, p. 13 and passim, and of "the *nouveaux riches*," Part II, p. 58 and passim. Also available in Paul M. Sweezy, chap. 9, "The American Ruling Class," Part I, in *The Present as History: Essays and Reviews on Capitalism and Socialism* (New York:

Monthly Review Press, 1953), pp. 120–129, and "The American Ruling Class," Part II, ibid., pp. 129–138, wherein the treatment of "the *nouveau riche*" is found in Part I, p. 124 and passim, and of "the *nouveaux riches*" in Part II, p. 130 and passim; all items in this paragraph also cited supra, pp. 109–110.

A more-explicit development of the reactionary political dispositions of "the . . . *nouveau riche Americanus*" is articulated in Leo Huberman and Paul M. Sweezy, "Review of the Month: The Roots and Prospects of McCarthyism," *Monthly Review: An Independent Socialist Magazine*, January 1954, pp. 417–434, and, especially, 422.

For a graphic portrayal of the frustrations of the new rich in regard to their lack of acceptance by the American ruling class, see F. Scott Fitzgerald, *The Great Gatsby* (New York: Charles Scribner's Sons, 1953).

An excellent depiction of psychological authority within the American ruling class itself is found in John O'Hara, *Ten North Frederick* (New York: Random House, 1955).

12. Cf., Paul N. Goldstene, "Theft as the Basis of American Public Policy: An Instructive Instance (1985)," in Paul N. Goldstene, *Democracy in America, Sardonic Speculations: Three Essays with a Postscript on Equal Opportunity* (Davis, CA: Bucknell House, 1991), pp. 53–63, and Goldstene, "Veblen's Theory of Value and the Problem of Revolution," pp. 507–520, and, especially, on the relationship of theories and doctrines of economic value to ideology and revolution, 515–517.

13. Cf., Arendt, *On Revolution*, p. 133 and passim.

14. Cf., Robert L. Heilbroner, *The Future as History: The Historic Currents of Our Time and the Direction in Which They Are Taking America* (New York: Harper and Brothers, 1960), chap. 1, "The Encounter with History," pp. 11–58, and, in particular, 57, and chap. 2, "The Closing-In of History," pp. 59–114.

15. Cf., Karl Marx, *Wage-Labour and Capital*, with an intro. by Frederick Engels (New York: International Publishers, Little Marx Library, 1933), especially chap. 7, "The General Law that Determines the Rise and Fall of Wages and Profits," pp. 36–38, and chap. 8, "The Interests of Capital and Wage-Labour Are Diametrically Opposed—Effect of Growth of Productive Capital on Wages," pp. 39–42, and Karl Marx, *Capital: A Critique of Political Economy*, ed. by Frederick Engels, trans. from the third German ed. by Samuel Moore and Edward Aveling, 3 vols. (New York: International Publishers, 1967), vol. 1, "The Process of Capitalist Production," especially chap. 18, "Various Formulae for the Rate of Surplus-Value," pp. 531–534.

16. The selling power of the one or the few which, in the parlance of economists, find their counterparts in "monopsony" and "oligopsony," the buying power of the one or the few, terms that are evidently too ugly to be generally employed.

17. Garry Wills, *Nixon Agonistes: The Crisis of the Self-Made Man* (Boston: Houghton Mifflin Co., 1970), Part One, "The Moral Market (Ralph Waldo

Emerson)," pp. 1–186, Part Two, "The Economic Market (Adam Smith)," pp. 187–316, Part Three, "The Intellectual Market (John Stuart Mill)," pp. 317–416, and Part Four, "The Political Market (Woodrow Wilson)," pp. 417–495.

18. For the basis of this perception, see Adolf A. Berle, Jr. and Gardiner C. Means, *The Modern Corporation and Private Property* (New York: The Macmillan Co., 1932), and James Burnham, *The Managerial Revolution: What Is Happening in the World* (New York: The John Day Co., 1941).

19. Cf., Galbraith, *New Industrial State*, on "The Technostructure," p. 71 and passim, capitalized for emphasis in the original in its first usage, and, especially, chap. 6, "The Technostructure," pp. 60–71, chap. 8, "The Entrepreneur and the Technostructure," pp. 86–97, and chap. 13, "Motivation and the Technostructure," pp. 149–158.

20. Cf., Adolf A. Berle, Jr., *The 20th Century Capitalist Revolution* (New York: Harcourt, Brace and World, 1954), wherein "the modern corporation," p. 9, is conceived of as "a social institution in the context of a revolutionary century," p. 24, and, more generally, 9 and passim, a phenomenon which is central to "the revolutionary capitalism of the mid-twentieth century," p. 9, although how corporate production is transformed into a variation of "capitalism" is not clear. However, also see Adolf A. Berle, Jr., *Power Without Property: A New Development in American Political Economy* (New York: Harcourt, Brace and Co., 1959), especially pp. 19 and 26–27, and Adolf A. Berle, *The American Economic Republic* (New York: Harcourt, Brace and World, 1963), especially p. vii and passim, and, more generally, chap. 1, "The Fragmentation of Economic Concepts: Property in Analysis," pp. 19–35, chap. 4, "The 'Free Market'—Friend or Menace?," pp. 76–84, chap. 6, "Assumption of Responsibility by the Political State," pp. 95–99, chap. 9, "The Controlled Markets," pp. 137–144, chap. 10, "The Free-Market Sector: Industry and Its Concentration," pp. 145–162, chap. 12, "The Welfare State: The Socialized Sector," pp. 176–185, and "Conclusion," pp. 213–218, wherein some effort is made to distinguish capitalism from a corporate order.

21. The best-known formulation of this is found in Grant McConnell, *Private Power and American Democracy* (New York: Alfred A. Knopf, 1967), p. 5 and passim, and, especially, chap. 5, "Private Government," pp. 119–154, although McConnell makes no claim that the formulation is of his own invention, ibid., p. 129. For an earlier use of this term, cf., Arthur S. Miller, "Private Governments and the Constitution," in Andrew Hacker (ed.), *The Corporation Take-Over*, The Center for the Study of Democratic Institutions (New York: Harper and Row Publishers, 1964), pp. 122–149, and, especially, "private governments," p. 131. Also cf., R. Jeffrey Lustig, *Corporate Liberalism: The Origins of Modern American Political Theory, 1890–1920* (Berkeley: University of California Press, 1982), especially Part Two, "The Emergence of Corporate Liberalism," pp. 107–264, and, in particular, chap. 5, "The

United States Incorporated: The Group Vision," pp. 109–149, and James Weinstein, *The Corporate Ideal in the Liberal State* (Boston: Beacon Press, 1968). Further, of course, and more cogently in terms of influence on the thinking of the 1960s, cf., C. Wright Mills, *White Collar: The American Middle Classes* (New York: Oxford University Press, 1953), wherein the perspective of an absorption of public policy into corporate interests is present throughout, and Mills, *Power Elite*, and, especially, for a summation of the argument, chap. 12, "The Power Elite," pp. 269–297.

Of further interest here, especially in regard to what extent a free market was ever a reality in the United States, are Mills, *White Collar*, pp. 15–23, and, in particular, 22–23, and John Kenneth Galbraith, *American Capitalism: The Concept of Countervailing Power* (Boston: Houghton Mifflin Co., 1956), chap. 3, "The Problem of Power," pp. 24–31, and, in particular, 24–28, and chap. 4, "The Abandonment of the Model," pp. 32–49.

22. Arendt, *On Revolution*, pp. 219–220.

23. Milton Friedman, *Capitalism and Freedom*, with the assistance of Rose D. Friedman (Chicago: The University of Chicago Press, 1962).

Chapter 8

1. As suggested in Al Richmond, *A Long View from the Left: Memoirs of an American Revolutionary* (Boston: Houghton Mifflin Co., 1973), p. 38.

2. On this, cf., Niles Eldredge and Stephen Jay Gould, "Speciation: Punctuated Equilibria: An Alternative to Phyletic Gradualism," in Part III, "Populations and Evolution," pp. 61–145, in J.M. Schopf (ed.), *Models in Paleobiology* (San Francisco: Freeman, Cooper and Co., 1972), pp. 82–115; Stephen Jay Gould and Niles Eldredge, "Punctuated Equilibria: The Tempo and Mode of Evolution Reconsidered," *Paleobiology*, Spring 1977, pp. 115–151; and Stephen Jay Gould, "Life in a Punctuation," *Natural History*, October 1992, pp. 10–21.

3. The recent academic popularity, especially among liberals, of Francis Fukuyama, *The End of History and the Last Man* (New York: The Free Press, 1992), is instructive. Also see Francis Fukuyama, "The End of History?," *The National Interest*, Summer 1989, pp. 3–18.

4. Cf., the development of the classical Greek idea of "*thymos*" as the major theme in Fukuyama, *End of History*, p. xvi and passim, a need which inspires human beings to "seek recognition of their own worth, or of the people, things, or principles that they invest with worth," ibid., p. xvii. As employed here, however, this motivation typifies only "certain human beings" who will, ideally, strive for the "things" of material wealth in the contemporary world, wherein the dangers of war have rendered a military expression of unequal attainment no longer rational, ibid., p. xxiii, and, especially, Part V, "The Last Man," pp. 283–339. Paralleling earlier conten-

tions about "the end of ideology," such an argument is useful for understanding this element within the liberal perspective. In this regard, the conception of *thymos* is also notably similar to the assumptions about human passions and appetites that invariably infuse the doctrine of capitalism, cf., for instance, John Adams, "Discourses on Davila," in Charles Francis Adams (ed.), *Works of John Adams*, vol. 6, in particular pp. 232 and, more generally, 232–235 and passim, cited supra, p. 116, n. 1.

    5. Brinton, *Anatomy of Revolution*, p. 203 and passim, and, especially, chap. 8, "Thermidor," pp. 205–236.

    6. Ibid., pp. 203, 17, and, more generally, for a view of the possible, and plainly very minimal, systemic benefits of revolution, 17 and passim.

    Accordingly, "we shall regard revolutions as a kind of fever," ibid., p. 16, and, "in terms of our conceptual scheme, we shall have to call Thermidor a convalescence from the fever of revolution," p. 205.

    Although "this is by no means to say . . . that what men think is of no importance," ibid., p. 247, the essential futility of revolutions results from "the fact . . . that . . . *sentiments* . . . are nearly constant; only . . . *ideas* . . . are variable, and in the long run the constant prevails," p. 246, a reality that, for Brinton, is evidently causal to "the conservative and routine-loving nature of the bulk of human beings" as well as to the "strong . . . habits of obedience in most of them," p. 253. The elitism here expressed is quite relevant to the discussion in ibid., p. 39 and passim, and, especially, 45, 46, 50–52, and 59, cited supra, p. 112, n. 7. Brinton consistently melds the idea of an "elite" into that of a "class," as previously suggested, supra, p. 112, n. 7.

    Also, note the comparison to "thunderstorms," which, indeed, may be "useful," ibid., p. 6 and passim, cited supra, p. 112, n. 7, but are, of course, of relatively short duration. For further employment of this metaphor, see ibid., pp. 10 and 14–15.

    Cf., the "fanatic," ibid., p. 114 and passim, as well as "Marxists," p. 18 and passim, "Communists," p. 22 and passim, "Jacobins," p. 96 and passim, and the translation of "Marxists" p. 243 and passim, into a vulgar Marxism, along with those who are "extremist," p. 22 and passim, "radical," p. 41 and passim, considered to be "red," p. 93 and passim, or are on "the Left," p. 97 and passim, which are types, augmented by the "radical extreme," p. 59 and passim, and "the professional radical," p. 110 and passim, that are more or less functional equivalencies which incite the "mob," p. 84 and passim, lead to "the rule of the extremists," p. 254 and passim, and, ultimately, yield a "Reign of Terror," p. 17 and passim, usually capitalized for emphasis in the original throughout, and, more generally, chap. 6, "The Accession of the Extremists," pp. 148–175, and chap. 7, "Reigns of Terror and Virtue," pp. 176–204. All in all, an impressive display of what will become the vocabulary of Cold-War scholarship.

    On the "Restoration," see ibid., p. 15 and passim, capitalized for emphasis in the original throughout.

The perception of revolutions which Brinton articulates frequently permeates novels drawn from discrete convolutions of contemporary history. Among the most influential, although with a good deal of ambivalence, are Arthur Koestler, *Darkness at Noon*, trans. by Daphne Hardy (New York: The Macmillan Co., 1941), and, with somewhat less ambivalence, Andre Malraux, *Man's Fate (La Condition Humaine)*, trans. by Haakon M. Chevalier, The Modern Library (New York: Random House, Modern Library College Editions, 1961). The same perspective is often also expressed through a literary genre that might be thought of as science fiction, probably the best known of which are, Jack London, *The Iron Heel*, intro. by H. Bruce Franklin (Westport, CT: Lawrence Hill and Co., 1980); Aldous Huxley, *Brave New World* (New York: Harper and Brothers, 1946); and George Orwell, *Nineteen Eighty-Four* (New York: Harcourt, Brace and Co., 1949), as well as through caricature, the most popular of which is probably George Orwell, *Animal Farm* (New York: Harcourt, Brace and Co., 1946).

It is of interest, however, that such works of apparent despair are usually written by people who continue to be committed to a fundamental systemic transition, eventuating in a literature less of resignation than of disappointment.

7. Brinton, *Anatomy of Revolution*, chap. 9, "Summary of the Work of Revolutions," pp. 237–264, and, in particular, 246 and 260, cited supra, p. 113, n. 9. Such a possibility is made even more explicit in ibid., "Epilogue: 1964," pp. 263–271, and, in particular, 268, wherein it is referred to as "this great master revolution" within which "there are very different constituent revolutions," p. 268.

8. In regard to the episodic character of the possibilities of revolutionary action, cf., Leo Huberman and Paul M. Sweezy, "Lessons of Soviet Experience," *Monthly Review: An Independent Socialist Magazine*, November 1967, pp. 18–19 and passim.

9. G.W.F. Hegel, *The Phenomenology of Mind*, trans. with an intro. and by J.B. Baille, 2nd ed., rev. and corrected throughout, Muirhead Library of Philosophy (London: George Allen and Unwin, 1949), chap. 4, "The Truth Which Conscious Certainty of Self Realizes," pp. 217–267, and, especially, Part A, "Independence and Dependence of Self-Consciousness: Lordship and Bondage," pp. 228–240.

10. Cf., Fromm, *Anatomy of Human Destructiveness*, wherein "power *over* people" is distinguished from "the power *to be*," while noting that there is a persistent attempt "to smuggle in the praise of 'power over'" by identifying "it with 'power to,'" p. 296. In any event, such an attempt is not being made here. Also see ibid., pp. 235–267 and passim, and Erich Fromm, *Man for Himself: An Inquiry into the Psychology of Ethics* (New York: Henry Holt and Co., An Owl Book, 1990), p. 88 and passim.

11. A graphic portrayal of this position is found in John Steinbeck, *Cannery Row* (New York: Bantam Books, 1972), especially p. 1.

Chapter 9

1. Cf., Norman Jacobson, *Pride and Solace: The Function and Limits of Political Theory* (Berkeley: University of California Press, 1978), p. 10 and passim.

2. Cf., Hannah Arendt, "On Violence," in Hannah Arendt, *Crises of the Republic* (San Diego: Harcourt, Brace and Jovanovich, Publishers, A Harvest, Harcourt Brace and Jovanovich Book, 1969), pp. 103–198, especially 139–146, and, most particularly, 140–141 and 144–145, n. 67, and Arendt, *On Revolution*, pp. 149–150.

3. Samuel D. Warren and Louis D. Brandeis, "The Right to Privacy," *Harvard Law Review* 4 (1890): 193.

4. Erich Fromm, *Marx's Concept of Man*, with a trans. of Karl Marx, *Economic and Philosophical Manuscripts*, by T.B. Bottomore, Milestones of Thought (New York: Continuum, A Frederick Ungar Book, 1992), wherein this is expressed as a matter of man "grasping the world productively, and thus making it his own," p. 29 and passim. For a more developed idea of what is intended here, see ibid., Part 4, "The Nature of Man," pp. 24–43, and, especially, section 2, "Man's Self-Activity," pp. 26–43. Accordingly, "man is alive only inasmuch as he is productive, inasmuch as he grasps the world outside of himself in the act of expressing his own specific human powers, and of grasping the world with these powers," ibid., p. 29, while human progress is that which moves people toward becoming "productively related to the whole world," p. 82.

More generally, cf., Fromm, *Man for Himself*, especially chap. 3, "Human Nature and Character," pp. 38–117, and, in particular, Part 3, "The Productive Orientation," pp. 82–107. Also, on "productive thinking" as an attempt to get beyond appearances to an understanding of a deeper reality, as well as on the opposition of such thinking to "the . . . process of bureaucratization" and its central connection to "the history of science," c.f., Erich Fromm, "The Crisis of Psychoanalysis," in *The Crisis of Psychoanalysis: Essays on Freud, Marx, and Social Psychology* (New York: Henry Holt and Co., An Owl Book, 1991, p.23. Thus productive behavior would be in essential accord with the more profound domains of scientific achievement.

5. Richard K. Matthews, *The Radical Politics of Thomas Jefferson: A Revisionist View* (Lawrence, KA: University Press of Kansas, 1986), pp. viii and passim and 125. Although this is in reference to "political theory," ibid., p. vii and passim, its relevance to scientific theory is plain throughout.

6. A creative and very useful formulation of this, applied to the argument of Hannah Arendt, is found in Catherine Nelson, "Science in Political Theory: The Search for Revolution," (working title), unpublished manuscript.

7. See "Appendix: A Note on 'Elite' and 'Social Class' as Conceptual Frameworks," supra, pp. 105–110.

8. Cf., Goldstene, *Collapse of Liberal Empire*, especially Part I, "Tradition," pp. 1–32, and Part III, "Renewal," pp. 89–127, and Goldstene, *Bittersweet Century*.

9. One exception to this was Galbraith, *New Industrial State*, especially chap. 23, "Education and Emancipation," pp. 370–378, chap. 24, "The Political Lead," pp. 379–387, and chap. 25, "The Future of the Industrial System," pp. 388–399 and passim, and, in particular, 399, but this came too late in the decade, and was probably too subtle a formulation, to influence the thinking of the time to any noticeable extent. Much more popular were works such as Herbert Marcuse, *One-Dimensional Man: Studies in the Ideology of Advanced Industrial Society* (Boston: Beacon Press, 1964), wherein the usual conflation of science and technology is central to the argument, as it continues to be central to the perspective of the political Left within the Western world.

10. Fromm, *Anatomy of Human Destructiveness*, in particular, pp. 235–267, cited supra, p. 128, n. 10. Also, cf., Erich Fromm, *Beyond the Chains of Illusion: My Encounter with Marx and Freud* (New York: Simon and Schuster, A Touchstone Book, 1962), pp. 74 and passim and 180 and passim; Erich Fromm, "Medicine and the Ethical Problem of Modern Man," in Fromm, *Dogma of Christ*, pp. 173–194, and, in particular, 182 and passim; Erich Fromm, chap. 5, "Let Man Prevail," in Erich Fromm, *On Disobedience: And Other Essays* (New York: The Seabury Press, 1981), pp. 58–74, and, especially, p. 70 and passim; and Erich Fromm, chap. 19, "Sex and Character," in *The Family: Its Function and Destiny*, rev. ed., Science of Culture Series, planned and ed. by Ruth Nanda Anshen, 8 vols. (New York: Harper and Brothers, Publishers, 1959), vol. 1, pp. 399–419, and, especially, 403.

Chapter 10

1. Fromm, *Anatomy of Human Destructiveness*, wherein "optimism is an alienated form of faith, pessimism an alienated form of despair," pp. 436, and, more generally, 436–438, and Fromm, chap. 9, "The Psychological Problems of Aging," in Fromm, *On Disobedience*, pp. 120–135, and, in particular, 125, 135, and, more generally, 125 and passim.

2. Cf., "the ideological veil with which society conceals the true nature of political relations," Hans J. Morgenthau, "Power as a Political Concept," in *Approaches to the Study of Politics: Twenty-Two Contemporary Essays Exploring the Nature of Politics and Methods by Which It Can Be Studied*, ed. by Roland Young (Evanston, IL: Northwestern University Press, 1958), p. 73, and, more generally, 72–73 and passim.

3. Cf., Sheldon S. Wolin, *Politics and Vision: Continuity and Innovation in Western Political Thought* (Boston: Little, Brown and Co., 1960), chap. 9, "Liberalism and the Decline of Political Philosophy," pp. 286–351.

4. Cf., Arendt, "On Violence," pp. 132–133.

5. Cf., Wolfe, *Limits of Legitimacy*, pp. 341–342, cited supra, p. 119, n. 6.

6. In, for instance, Thomas Jefferson, "Jefferson to Adams," Monticello, June 15, 1813, in *The Adams-Jefferson Letters: The Complete Correspondence Between Thomas Jefferson and Abigail and John Adams*, ed. by Lester J. Cappon, 2 vols. (Chapel Hill, NC: The University of North Carolina Press, 1959), vol. 2, 1812–1826, p. 332; Thomas Jefferson, "To Samuel A. Smith," Monticello, September 21, 1814, in *The Works of Thomas Jefferson*, collected and ed. by Paul Leicester Ford, Federal Edition, 12 vols. (New York: G.P. Putnam's Sons, The Knickerbocker Press, 1905), vol. 11, pp. 427–430; and Thomas Jefferson, "To Roger Weightman," Monticello, June 24, 1826, ibid., vol. 12, pp. 476–477, and, especially, 477, which, incidently, is apparently the last letter Jefferson was to write. In regard to the contention being made here, the first letter cited is clear enough, while the second really implies the point, and the third makes it quite plain.

Bibliography*

There are many histories of "revolutions" but a paucity of works that actually attempt to formulate a theory of revolution. Among contemporary political scientists concerned with such theories, most would probably agree that the following titles are indispensable.

Crane Brinton, *The Anatomy of Revolution.*

James C. Davies, "The J-Curve of Rising and Declining Satisfactions as a Cause of Some Great Revolutions and a Contained Rebellion," in Hugh Davis Graham and Ted Robert Gurr (eds.), *The History of Violence in America: Historical and Comparative Perspectives,* pp. 690–730.

John Dunn, *Modern Revolutions: An Introduction to the Analysis of a Political Phenomenon.*

Ted Robert Gurr, *Why Men Rebel.*

Samuel P. Huntington, *Political Order in Changing Societies.*

Chalmers Johnson, *Revolutionary Change.*

Theda Skocpol, *States and Social Revolutions: A Comparative Analysis of France, Russia, and China.*

Charles Tilly, "Does Modernization Breed Revolution?," *Comparative Politics,* April 1973, pp. 425–447.

A very personal list of works that have centrally informed the argument in this book.

Maxwell Anderson, "Key Largo."

———, "Winterset."

Hannah Arendt, *On Revolution.*

Charles A. Beard, *An Economic Interpretation of the Constitution of the United States.*

Carl Becker, *The Heavenly City of the Eighteenth-Century Philosophers.*

*Since many of these references are found in various editions, except for journal citations publication details are omitted.

Daniel Bell, "The Background and Development of Marxian Socialism in the United States," in Drew Egbert and Stow Persons (eds.), *Socialism and American Life*, pp. 213–405.

Adolf A. Berle, Jr., *The 20th Century Capitalist Revolution*.

J. Bronowski, *Science and Human Values*.

W.R. Cash, *The Mind of the South*.

Ronald W. Clark, *Einstein: The Life and Times*.

Howard Fast, *Citizen Tom Paine*.

Erich Fromm, *The Anatomy of Human Destructiveness*.

John Kenneth Galbraith, *The New Industrial State*.

Walter Goldschmidt, *Man's Way: A Preface to the Understanding of Human Society*.

Louis Hartz, *The Liberal Tradition in America: An Interpretation of American Political Thought Since the Revolution*.

Franz Kafka, *The Castle*.

Archibald MacLeish, "America Was Promises (1939)."

Karl Marx, *Critique of the Gotha Programme*.

————, *Early Writings*, trans. and ed. by T. B. Bottomore.

Richard K. Matthews, *The Radical Politics of Thomas Jefferson: A Revisionist View*.

Fritz Pappenheim, *The Alienation of Modern Man: An Interpretation Based on Marx and Tönnies*.

Carl Sandburg, "The People, Yes."

Budd Schulberg, *What Makes Sammy Run?*

Robert Sherwood, "There Shall Be No Night."

C. P. Snow, *The Two Cultures and the Scientific Revolution*.

————, *The Physicists*.

Lincoln Steffens, *The Autobiography of Lincoln Steffens*.

John Steinbeck, "Viva Zapata!: The Screenplay."

Paul M. Sweezy, "The American Ruling Class," Parts I and II, *Monthly Review: An Independent Socialist Magazine*, May and June, 1951, pp. 10–17 and 58–64

Thorstein Veblen, *The Instinct of Workmanship and the State of the Industrial Arts*.

Garry Wills, *Nixon Agonistes: The Crisis of the Self-Made Man*.

Index